How Shall I Tell the Dog?

and other final musings

Miles Kington

Afterword by Caroline Kington

Newmarket Press

For Sophie, Tom, Isabel and Adam

First published in the U.S. in 2009 by Newmarket Press

First published in Great Britain in 2008 by Profile Books Ltd

This book is published in the United States of America.

First Edition

ISBN: 978-1-55704-841-7

10 9 8 7 6 5 4 3 2 1

Library of Congress Cataloging-in-Publication Data available upon
request.

Quantity Purchases

Companies, professional groups, clubs, and other organizations may
qualify for special terms when ordering quantities of this title. For
information, e-mail sales @newmarketpress.com or write to Special Sales,
Newmarket Press, 18 East 48th Street, New York, NY 10017; call (212)
832-3575 ext. 19 or 1-800-669-3903; FAX (212) 832-3629.

Text design by Sue Lamble

Manufactured in the United States of America.

www.newmarketpress.com

PART I

Facing the Mountain

A Good Idea

Dear Gill,

You asked me the other day if I had any ideas for books that I wanted to write, so I am writing back to you now to remind you that that was the first question you ever asked me when we first met nearly thirty years ago.

Actually, it wasn't quite the first question. The first question – and I cannot remember who asked it, you or me – was 'What on earth are we doing here?' That was because we were both guests at a *Private Eye* lunch at the Coach and Horses, in the upstairs room where all the hacks met once or twice a month to swap gossip about other hacks.

I think I know what I was doing there. I had been on the staff of *Punch* for fifteen years and had just resigned to go freelance. *Punch* and *Private Eye* were great rivals in those days, and although their cartoonists moved easily from one magazine to the other, there was no overlap of writers at all. If you wrote for *Punch*, you *never* wrote for *Private Eye*, and vice versa.

And within a month of leaving *Punch*, I was invited to a *Private Eye* lunch. I don't think for a moment I was being asked to contribute to *Private Eye*, which indeed I never have been. It was more like being welcomed across the Berlin Wall. I had defected from *Punch*, and the free world was giving me a free lunch. And all I can remember about it now was sitting next to you, and you not being at all sure what you were doing there, and you saying 'Well, if you're going freelance, have you any ideas for books you want to write?'

I did, as a matter of fact. (I think all freelance writers have stacks of unwritten books at the back of their minds, mostly impracticable and almost all destined never to be written.) And the one I was keenest to tell you about was my *World Atlas of Prejudice*.

This was a project for a global guide which would tell you immediately just what everyone in the world thought about everyone else. Well, not everyone. What the Austrians think about the Australians is of little interest to anyone, and people in Siberia never tell jokes about people in Patagonia.

And you don't really need a book to tell you what the French and the English think of each other, or the Irish and the English. Or the Americans and Canadians. Or the Australians and New Zealanders. We always tend to know what close neighbours think of each other. But as soon as it becomes a bit remote – even a tiny bit remote – we are floundering. What do the French think of the Spaniards? Do they have a pet name for each other, the way we call the French 'frogs' or Germans 'krauts'? The Italians and Spaniards – what do they think of each other? What do the Italians think of French driving? Are the British the only people in the world who think that the Germans get up at dawn to put their bathing towels on good bits of the poolside?

My book would explain all this.

I once read a book by Alistair Horne about South America in which he told a Chilean joke.

It went like this.

'A group of Chilean men are drinking in a bar and one says suddenly, "What would you do if you came home early one day and found your wife in bed with another man?" One of the other men says immediately, "I would go out and break every window in the US Embassy!"'

End of story.

Alistair Horne then explains the joke. The power of the USA is so all-pervasive in South America that they get the blame (and sometimes credit) for absolutely everything.

Now, you can't really laugh at a joke after it has been explained to you, but you can see why it is funny to other people, and that joke from Chile – the only Chilean joke I have ever heard – suddenly explained to me the love–hate relationship of the Latino and the gringo in a way I had never seen before.

I think I told you all this, and you thought it was a terrific idea for a book and asked me to write down a résumé of it, and I did, and you sold the idea to a publisher for a lot of money!

How I never wrote the book and how eventually we had to pay all the advance back is another story, but at least it proved that I could have good ideas for books. And you have been my agent ever since, and I am still trying to think of good ideas for books for you!

Love,
Miles

Cashing In on Cancer

Dear Gill,

About a year ago, I said I wanted to do another book. That is, I was going to write it and you were going to sell it.

Fine, you said. What kind of book?

A bestseller, I said. Something that will be so funny that everyone will buy it, even when it isn't Christmas, and which will bring back dignity to the Humour shelves in bookshops, which are presently occupied by miserable things called *Is It Me, Or Is Everywhere A Crap Town?* or *Why Are Penguins Camouflaged Like That, When There Aren't Any Head Waiters In The Antarctic?*

Fine, you said. Got any ideas?

One thing at a time, I said. First I get the urge to write the book. Which I have already got! Then later I get the idea for the book.

Fine, you said. Let me know when you have got a good idea for a book.

Well, I think I have now got a good idea for a book.

Which, oddly enough, was not one I thought of, but was given to me by a doctor, quite by accident.

As you know, I went into hospital last spring to have my liver looked at, because blood tests showed that my liver was misbehaving. Almost immediately they discovered the reason. I had contracted an unusual genetic disease called haemachromatosis, which makes it difficult for the body to absorb iron, so my bloodstream had become abnormally high in iron content.

(This might explain why I was being so often stopped by security people in airports. Even after I had emptied all my pockets and taken off all my metal accessories, I was still setting off the alarm when I went through the metal detector again. They could never find any reason for it. But it may have been the high metal content of my blood … at least, so I claimed in a piece I wrote about it at the time.)

Haemachromatosis is no big deal and can be cleared up by a programme of blood-letting. (Every time you lose the blood, the body makes some more, and the new blood is all iron-free.) But they then spotted some trouble in my bile duct and decided to insert a plastic pipe to open up a small blockage. Then they decided to take out my gall bladder. When they did that, they spotted some irregularities in my liver and pancreas, and decided to take some samples, and it was after looking closely at those that they decided I had got cancer. Nosey parkers.

Cancer of the pancreas, it was. This was unfortunate, because, as a doctor friend of mine said to me, 'That's not one of the nice ones.' Not much research work has been done on it, you can't operate on it, and even chemotherapy does little more than arrest the process.

So, at the age of sixty-six, I suddenly found that my expected life span of another twenty years at least had shrunk dramatically.

The surgeon who had operated on me was surprisingly upbeat.

'Don't think of yourself as dying,' he said. 'We are all dying anyway. Just think that you now know what you are going to die of. Up to now, it might have been a heart attack, or a stroke. But now we're pretty sure it's going to be cancer. Though not for ages, yet. With luck.'

The oncologist who did the follow-up chat was less upbeat.

'Statistically you will be doing well if you are still hale and hearty a year from now.'

That was a shock. It was what finally brought me up short. Till that moment, I had been unsure what to think. My mind was full of images of writers cut off in their prime, and of *La Dame aux Camélias*, and of having

9

to give up wine, and of seeing weeping relatives round my death bed – in other words, I was full of self-pity – but suddenly all this miasma of hand-wringing crystallised into one single thought: I did not have as much time left as I thought in which to do all the important things of life, such as:

1   Sorting out the family finances
2   Finally getting round to seeing *American Beauty*
3   Writing a book for you.

But it did dimly occur to me at last that I had the glimmerings of an idea for a book for you. People who have been told they have cancer are sometimes brave enough to start writing books about their experience, and how they came to terms with it. For instance, the chap who was married to Nigella Lawson, whose name I can never remember. He did it. He got the TV cameras in as well, I believe. There was a woman called Picardie too, wasn't there? Ruth? Something like that. And there was a French comedian called Pierre Desproges, who I always rather liked the sound of, because not only did he write funny stuff, he also had a weekly radio or TV spot in France on which he delivered his quirky views on the week's news, and in which his newly diagnosed cancer became a regular character. Until he died.

I also purchased a book while I was in Canada

called *Typing* by Matt Cohen. Matt Cohen was a not very old writer who had suddenly been given another six months to live before he died of lung cancer, and decided to spend the time writing his memoirs, *Typing*. It was brilliant.

Apart from the Cohen, I have never read any of these books. I tend to shy away from bad news. But I know that a writer wouldn't devote his last months to writing about cancer if there wasn't some money in it.

I'd like to do the same.

Mark you, I think phrases like 'cashing in on cancer' give quite the wrong impression.

What I mean is, 'making cancer work for its living'.

What do you think?

Love,
Miles

A Conversation with My Doctor

Dear Gill,

No, you are right. Although I had said I had come up with an idea for a book, I hadn't done anything of the sort. I had only come up with an idea for an idea for a book. I still have to think of an angle.

You ask me if I have mentioned this idea for an idea for a book to anyone. Yes, I have, but only to one person. To the oncologist at the hospital.

Actually, I think you would have been quite proud of my professionalism during our little interview. When he was patiently explaining to me the pros and cons of various treatments, and his views on alternative cancer treatments (described to me by one doctor I know as 'an expensive way of buying love'), he said at one point: 'Do you have any questions?'

I can never think of proper questions at that moment, except for cowardly ones ('Is it going to hurt a lot?') or unanswerable ones ('Will it stop me from playing the double bass?'), but this time I knew what I wanted to ask. I wanted to ask: 'Can I get a book out of this?'

I am experienced enough to know by now that you have to be a bit more oblique than that, especially when talking to amateurs, so I toned the question down and we had the following exchange:

Me: 'How many stages will this go through?'
Him: 'How do you mean – stages?'
Me: 'Well … how many chapter headings?'
Him: 'Chapter headings?'
Me: 'Yes. I mean, if one were, to take a wild example, writing a book about this experience, how many sections do you think it would fall into?'
Him: 'Sections?'
Me: 'Yes.'
Him: 'Well … Look, I'm going to reverse the normal pattern here, and *I* am going to ask *you* a question.'
Me: 'Fire away.'
Him: 'Are you *planning* to write a book about this?'
Me: 'It had occurred to me, yes …'
Him: 'I have to tell you I don't think you will have enough time to write a proper book about your cancer.'
Me: 'That's a bit unfair. You may be very good at giving people time limits when they are suffering from cancer, but I am not sure how much of an expert you

13

are when it comes to saying how long it takes to write a book.'

Him: 'No, perhaps not, but I know how long it takes to get to grips with a subject as complex as cancer, especially when new research is going on the whole time …'

Me: 'Research? No, no, no! You've got it all wrong! I'm not thinking of a textbook! I don't want to produce a research work on cancer! I'm only thinking of a personal journal!'

Him: 'Personal journal?'

Me: 'Yes.'

Him: 'I don't quite …'

Me: 'Well, writers quite like to turn their experiences into books, and that includes their illnesses. You know, like Dennis Potter did with his psoriasis in *The Singing Detective*. But it's more fashionable these days to turn it into a first-person account, as John Walsh did.'

Him: 'And that's what you're going to do?'

Me: 'I was thinking of it.'

Him: 'Well, good. That would be jolly good therapy, I would think.'

It wasn't till later that I realised he had obviously never heard of John Walsh, which was just as well, because I wasn't thinking of John Walsh at all. I was thinking of John Diamond, the late Mr Nigella Lawson.

Mark you, it was an understandable mistake on my part. John Walsh has written a series of amiable autobiographies, in each of which he has viewed the same lifespan through different prisms. Once as growing up with his favourite films. Once as growing up Irish in London, and therefore also with Catholicism. Once as something else quite different, I think, but I can't remember what. Once or twice a week in the *Independent* he continues an account of his life as a once-or-twice-a-week-in-the-*Independent* journalist. I would feel suitably downcast if John Walsh did really contract cancer, because sure as eggs are eggs, he would write a witty, sparkling, Catholic, Irish, film-loving book about his life with cancer, and get there before me, curse him.

The next time I met the oncologist, he asked me again if I had any questions.

Me: 'Yes. Are *you* writing a book about cancer?'
Him: 'Yes, I am. How on earth did you know that?'
Me: 'It was something you said last time. When you were anxious about me writing a book. You said you didn't think I would have enough time.'
Him: 'Well, I have been working on mine for twenty years already, and it's not nearly finished …'

No competition there, then. And a bit of a clue. He doesn't think I have another twenty years left. But

I never did either, even before I had cancer.

I see I haven't really come up with an idea for a book in this letter either.

Next time, then!

Love,
Miles

1,000 Places to See Before You Die

Dear Gill,

When you've been diagnosed with cancer (a phrase I still can't think of a good euphemism for, even though everyone I meet can think of a bad one), one of the most annoying books in the world suddenly turns out to be *1,000 Places to See Before You Die.*

Have you come across this?

It's a fat American paperback which lists a thousand of the most remarkable sights in the world, natural or man-made, from canyons to cathedrals.

We have had a copy of this book knocking around our hall for a year now, on the shelves where we tend to keep the travel guides. It was certainly there before the oncologist drew on his little black cap and pronounced sentence. Until that moment I quite approved of the idea of the book. Here we all were, with twenty or thirty more years to live, and it was about time we started concentrating on using those fallow years to get to places we have been too lazy, poor or blasé to have a look at so far.

1,000 Places to See Before You Die.

Ha ha. But very useful, and full of ideas.

When I learnt I'd got cancer, the book suddenly looked very different.

Threatening.

Humourless.

Grimly prescient.

1,000 Places to See Before You Die.

Nasty.

Fun-free.

Evil.

'We know you are going to die,' it seemed to say, 'and we know you haven't got anything like enough time to see a hundred worthwhile places, let alone a thousand, so you're up against it, aren't you, pal? A lot of drastic choosing and travelling to do, haven't you? You're going to have to decide what to see next while you're already en route to the previous place. And every time you browse through the book, trying to make up your mind, you're wasting the time and chance to see somewhere. Get a move on, because while you sit there dithering … Oops – there goes the Taj Mahal!'

It would be immensely satisfying if I could round up a few fellow sufferers to mount a law suit against this preposterous volume, put together by one

Patricia Schultz, and dubbed a 'No. 1 *New York Times* Bestseller', on the grounds that it caused intense suffering to those who are about to die and haven't a hope in hell of seeing all those places. Luckily for her, I have many enticing things to do with my remaining time; taking money from Miss P. Schultz and then handing it all straight over to my lawyers is not one of them. Are not one of them. Are not two of them.

Having browsed grimly through 'A Traveller's Life List', as la Schultz subtitles her remorseless catalogue of treasures, I am relieved to find that, were I to take this over-inflated travel magazine article seriously, I could do some crossing off the list already and reduce the number from a thousand to nearer nine hundred and ninety. Yes, I have been to one or two of Schultz's Sights already. Machu Picchu. Salisbury Cathedral. Wells Cathedral. The Schwe Dagon Pagoda in Rangoon. Loch Ness. The Moscow Underground … (Starting to run out now …)

Two of these I can even bracket together. In 1980 I was lucky enough to be taken by the BBC to Peru as the presenter of 'Three Miles High', one of the programmes in the *Great Railway Journeys* series. Our trip passed through Machu Picchu at one point, and allowed me to see the Lost City of the Incas and the legendary craftsmanship that fitted those great massive stones together so snugly, and all without the use of any adhesive.

'Is it not remarkable,' said an expert to me as we stood and surveyed the remains, 'that six hundred years ago another civilisation unknown to ours could construct something so brilliant?'

If he hadn't said it, I might have agreed with him.

As it was, the spirit of rebellion suddenly moved within me.

'No,' I said. 'Not really. At about the same time as they were building Machu Picchu, or even earlier, we in Britain had pretty much finished Salisbury Cathedral. Give me Salisbury Cathedral any day. It makes Machu Picchu look like a child's toy.'

How smug I felt. And I was right, of course. The main reason that Machu Picchu looks so good, apart from its dramatic position, is that you don't expect people in the South American jungle to be building stonework like that six hundred years ago, certainly not up a mountain, and you don't expect it to be lost for centuries until American adventurer Hiram Bingham blinks in the middle of a wood, and realises he is surrounded by some nice old remains and that from now on Yanks won't have to go to Europe for *all* their historical kicks any more.

It's still pretty basic stuff, Machu Picchu.

Imagine if you were stumbling through the forests of Peru and came across Salisbury Cathedral standing there, whole and entire, brightly maintained, with a notice at the door saying: 'While we do not charge for admission, we hope for a contribution of at least £5 from each person', *then* you would be entitled to say 'Holy Moley', have a small nervous breakdown, clasp cold flannels to your forehead, and phone everyone at home saying 'Look at *this* little photo I've just taken!', or whatever is your preferred reaction to joyous shock.

Salisbury Cathedral beats a full house, four queens, five aces and Machu Picchu.

(It was stressed to me in Peru that Machu Picchu was not actually the only Lost City of the Incas. I was also taken to see a place called Sacsahuamán, which is full of similarly amazing stonework and, being much less frequented by tourists, is much more tranquil and atmospheric. Oddly, it is not nearly so remote as Machu Picchu, being almost within walking distance of Cuzco. It reminds me that in Wiltshire local people will always advise you against going to the full tourist horror of Stonehenge and urge you instead to visit Avebury, which is not quite so sensational a Stone Age site but more attractive and, being enmeshed in a village, much less like a museum site, and – hey! I wonder if there's a pattern here? Do you think there are enough places throughout the world which are as good as their more famous counterparts to justify a book on them? A book called *1,000 Places to See Before You Die Which Are Pretty Much as Good as Patty Schultz's*

Top Thousand and Not Half As Crowded? Just a thought …)

The odd thing is that I do live in Wiltshire myself and am barely an hour from Salisbury, yet I think I have been inside Salisbury Cathedral only once in my life. I have often seen it from the distance, and occasionally from close up, if you can ever properly see a cathedral from close up, and it really is the most extraordinary, floating, extra-terrestrial, perfect, fantastical stone space ship you could want. Yet I could only be bothered to go in it once. And that was while I still lived in London, and was just passing through Wiltshire!

That's the other thing they say, of course, that people who live nearby never go. It is legendarily rare to find a Londoner who has been to the Tower of London (and then only if taking a visitor there). I have in-laws called Keith and Belinda who live less than an hour's drive from Niagara Falls, and boy, are they sick to death with taking people to Niagara Falls. They couldn't care less if they never see the Falls again. When people come to stay, they now tell them: 'Go and see Niagara Falls if you like, but don't expect us to come along to see the bloody thing!' (Things? Thing?)

There might be an idea for a series of books here, introducing people who live in a place to what *they* should go and see. *London for Londoners*. *The*

Billericay That Nobody Knows. The Liverpool That Nobody Likes …

Anything in this letter appeal to you?

Love,
Miles

PS How about *A Hundred Things to Do Before You Die?*

Niagara Falls

Dear Gill,

Talking of Niagara Falls, I suddenly remembered that while I was reading a volume of Tchaikovsky's *Diaries* (as research for my epoch-making play *The Death of Tchaikovsky – a Sherlock Holmes Mystery*), I came across an unexpected episode in the Russian composer's life when he also became a tourist visitor to Niagara Falls. He had gone to America in 1891 to conduct the very first concert in Carnegie Hall and as part of the process of being lionised, he was taken on a solemn visit to the great Falls. How strange to think of the exotic Slav doing something so very modern and American. (All I can remember of his account now is his extremely politically incorrect distress at there being so many Jewish stall-holders doing business beside the Falls.)

But I also remember thinking that there must have been so many famous people who have been to the Falls over the years that there might be enough material for a small anthology in their various reactions. I know that Oscar Wilde went there, and made one or two good remarks about the Falls. And Rupert Brooke went there too, and wrote a whole article about the Falls. This turns up in his very interesting but now quite forgotten volume of travel pieces from America called *Letters From America*. (Yes, it wasn't the dreadful Alistair Cooke, as Geoffrey Wheatcroft insists on calling him, who invented that title.) And I am sure there would be a quotable quote from Alex Atkinson's rollicking *By Rocking Chair Across America*, a 1950s publication which has wonderful drawings by Ronald Searle.

(This equally forgotten travel classic has a noble beginning, perhaps the best beginning of any travel book ever written. It says: 'Many books on America have been written by people who had hardly spent more than two or three weeks in the country. This one is different. It is written by someone who has never been there in his life.')

Yep, a collection of different perceptions of the great Niagara Falls, that's my idea.

Bet you never saw that one coming.

A sure-fire winner if ever I heard one.

Let me know what you think.

Love,
Miles

PS I have just located my Rupert Brooke book, and looked up his description of Niagara Falls. It's not very good. He is overpowered by the effort of describing the power and force of the cascade, and disappears in a hissing, mighty maelstrom of adjectives and shiny adverbs. But his description of the touts who ply their trade on shore is quite good.

A Hundred Things to Do Before You Die

Dear Gill,

I see that in a previous letter I proposed the idea of a book to be written by me called *A Hundred Things to Do Before You Die*.

Yes, you may object that this sounds much too like P. Schultz's *1,000 Places to See Before You Die*, the No 1 *New York Times* bestseller.

It may well do.

There is, however, a vital difference between her book and mine.

P. Schultz is not interested in people doing things. She is only interested in people going to see places.

She wants her readers to buy an airline ticket, go halfway round the world, see Wells Cathedral and go home again.

(I abbreviate.)

She does not suggest ways of filling in time en route to Wells, or on the way back from Wells, or even, much, while at Wells.

It is, I am afraid, a very American vision of the world, as a series of sights to be ticked off one by one.

My idea may sound similar but it is quite different insofar as it involves *doing* things.

Not doing things in the sense of doing a bungee jump or white water rafting, which in its own way is just as bad as going halfway round the world to see Angkor Wat.

Doing things in the sense of finally getting round to doing all those things you'd always wished you could do, but never did master.

Without leaving home.

An example?

Certainly.

Whistling with two fingers in your mouth.

It was always a great regret to me that I grew up not being able to do that, while people who were much stupider than I was had no trouble at all just sticking fingers in their mouth and breaking the sound barrier. I could whistle ordinarily easily enough, and do tunes and everything. But I couldn't emit that piercing whistle which stopped taxis in their tracks, attracted the attention of everyone with earshot and brought down prices of property in the neighbourhood.

Then one day in my twenties I found an article in *Esquire* magazine called something like: 'Your Very Last Chance To Learn How To Put Your Fingers In

Your Mouth (But Wash Them First) And Whistle Like An Errand Boy, Just As You Always Wanted To', and I realised that it *was* my last chance, and I grimly cut the piece out and started practising. It's a hit and miss process, but I persevered and one day I flukily got a loud whistle while pushing the tip of my tongue back, and then I got it again, and over a period of time I eliminated the errors until now, in my sixties, I can put two fingers in my mouth and get that ear-quaking blast nine times out of ten.

I don't do it very often. Sometimes to try to flag a taxi down. Sometimes to tell my wife where I am in a supermarket. Very occasionally to attract people's attention as they are about to wander out on to that harmless-looking bit of grass which, did they but know it, leads to an unsuspected 300-foot cliff fall or conceals a glutinous swamp from which no one has ever clambered alive (the trick is to leave the whistle to the last possible moment, as otherwise people think you are just interfering and being bossy). The important thing is that, whatever the motive for my shrill whistling, someone standing nearby always says: 'God, I've always wanted to be able to do that!' and they don't mean to rescue people from certain death, they mean they want to be able to whistle with their fingers in their mouth. Sometimes everyone in earshot says this. Occasionally someone actually says: '*Please* teach me how to do that!'

Yes, the world is full of people who wish they could put two fingers in their mouth and a moment later be heard as far away as Ealing.

(My daughter Sophie is even better at this than I am. She can put two fingers *of the same hand* in her mouth and get the whistle going. I can only do it with two hands. That is how I would have to teach it, maybe even risking lawsuits from one-handed whistlers who saw me as the Patricia Schultz of the whistling world.)

What is clear from all this is that lots of people, right through their lives, go on wishing they could do the big two-fingered whistle and would pay good money to learn how to do so.

Ah, if only they could buy a book which told them simply and clearly how to do it, wouldn't they shell out the money?

Especially if it told them how to do ninety-nine other things as well, for the same price?

Dear Miles, I hear you say, Can there possibly be ninety-nine other things like that as well?

Of course there are, dear Gill! you hear me reply, in the immortally unctuous tones of an author allaying an agent's doubts.

For instance, yodelling.

I can do the big two-fingered whistle, but no one has ever taught me how to do that register change while singing, that slip from normal to falsetto and back which makes you sound like a Swiss busker or like Billy Connolly doing his ten-minute routine about learning how to yodel. I have not often wanted to know how to do it, but when I have wanted to know, I have wanted to know very badly.

And if I read *A Hundred Things to Do Before You Die*, by Miles Kington, I would find out.

Other things covered in this sensationally vital new volume include such techniques and topics as:
'How a Crossword Clue Works.'
'Why the Ref Blew the Whistle.'
'How to Cut Your Thumb In Half, Using Your
    Opposite Forefinger as The Knife.'
'How to Stick a Stamp on the Ceiling From Where
    You are Sitting, Using Only a 50p Coin (and a
    Stamp).'
'How to Pronounce "Macho" and "Chorizo"
    Properly, Unlike Mark Lawson.'
'How to Send Postcards Home To Your Mother
    Country.'
'How to Swear in Other Languages.'
'The Do's and Don'ts of Wearing a Crucifix.'
'The Secret of Steaming Open an Envelope (Do It at
    the Bottom).'
'How to Do a Handstand.'
'And a Cartwheel.'
'How to Catch a Barman's Eye.'
'How to Dive Into a Swimming Pool.'

'Making a Shrieking Sound with a Blade of Grass.'
'Hand-carving your own Wooden Date Retrieving
    Fork To Replace the Horrible Plastic One They
    Give You in Boxes of Moroccan Dates These Days.'
'How to Fix a Ballcock ...'

Ah!

There is a bit of personal experience attached to this last one.

In the 1970s I lived in a modern block of flats in Ladbroke Grove, on the ground floor. There were about ten flats above me, all in identical format. The bathroom was in the same place in each flat. In each bathroom there was a lavatory, with an overflow which led to an outside pipe. Looking up from my garden, you could see nine pipes one above the other, which would only come into action if there was an overflow (of clean water) from the cistern in the loo.

It happened one night. A cistern somewhere upstairs started to malfunction. All I knew about it was that it suddenly started to rain in our garden. I rushed out to see why we had such a localised rain-storm and spotted that it was all coming from four floors up, so I tore up the stairs and knocked at the fourth floor to tell the occupant that something very odd was going on. She was dumbfounded. I was a total stranger (we were all strangers to each other in the block) and yet I seemed to know that her loo was misbehaving. Was I not rather a burglar tricking my way in? A rapist? A lavatory fetishist?

Eventually I managed to get her to look at her overflow pipe, which was indeed overflowing, and then we had a look inside her cistern. I could see that the water was coming into the cistern to refill it. I could see that the ballcock had not quite got to the top on its floating arm. I could work out that what needed to be done was …

Well, never mind what needed to be done, but I bent the arm, or released something, and stopped the overflow overflowing, and we parted on the best of terms, and all was as before.

Until the next flat developed an overflow deluge.

And I had to go up and talk my way into the next cistern, and deal with it.

And again, and again and again, over the years.

In every case I managed to mend it.

I met lots of my neighbours.

I streamlined my invasion technique until instead of explaining at great length how I lived on the ground floor and there was water falling on our garden, and if only she would let me look at the ballcock, etc., etc., I merely brushed past the tenant saying, 'Ballcock trouble, emergency plumber, let me through,' and got it done in a minute flat.

I began to get a bit of a reputation as a whiz with

plumbing, and total strangers would sometimes call from upstairs asking me to look at their boilers, or central heating.

This was beyond me.

I had mastered ballcocks, and that is all I intended to do.

After all, their central heating was no danger to my garden.

Still, it took me weeks and months of trial and error just to work out how ballcocks behave, and I think that if I had had *A Hundred Things to Do Before You Die* by Miles Kington to hand, I would have blessed its presence.

As indeed would, now, lots of people who are conscious of all those little techniques they have not mastered in life, and all for the want of a little trying and the right book.

Sounds like a bestseller to me.

What do you think?

Love,
Miles

Eleanor Bron and the Art of Mending a Puncture

Dear Gill,

The whole point of *A Hundred Things to Do Before You Die* (by Miles Kington) would be that we all have little unclimbed peaks within us waiting for our own little personal Union Jacks to be planted on the peak. Nobody has to go climbing Everest to get that achievement. You may only have to learn how to tie a bow tie or, in the case of a woman, toss a coin. Women very seldom, in my experience, have mastered the art of putting a coin on their thumb and tossing it to start a Cup Final. They hardly ever need to, of course. But very occasionally, like when starting a game of boules, or settling a family argument, they really do need to. I have seen grown women reduced nearly to tears by not being able to balance a coin on a thumb …

Here is a real-life example of a real woman who needed a real personal accomplishment and let herself down when it mattered.

Years and years ago I was asked by the *Sunday*

Times to review a book by Eleanor Bron, the actress, called *Life and Other Punctures*. Bron had gone on a bicycling holiday in Northern France and been persuaded to write it up as a small travel book. I looked forward to reading it, as I wanted to know more about Northern France and was keen on bicycling, even if I was mostly limited to my daily cycle trip from Notting Hill to Fleet Street and back.

Well, I enjoyed the book, but I didn't learn much about France or bicycling for the very simple reason that Eleanor Bron was not much of a bicyclist and got hardly anywhere at all in Northern France. She kept having punctures. She did not know how to mend punctures. So every time she got a puncture, she had to push her machine along miles of empty French road till she found a garage, a bike shop, a friendly bicyclist or a hotel with a handyman.

I sympathised with her over the punctures because even when you think you know how, they're not that easy to fix. I learnt through trial and error, and with hints from my local bike shop, E. J. Barnes of Westbourne Grove (advt). I learnt that you have to leave the sticky solution to dry a lot longer than you think before it's ready to receive the patch. I learnt not to put patches on the wrong way round. I learnt that you can take the outer tube off with tyre levers, but you mustn't use tyre levers to put it back on, because of the danger of pinching the now half-inflated inner tube, which to my shame I have done now and then …

By the time I came to review Bron's book, I was pretty good at mending punctures, and could also replace gear and brake cables. I couldn't do spoke replacement or fiddle with derailleur gears, but punctures I could do, *and Eleanor Bron, a famous actress, couldn't!* How I would like to have taken her in hand, or even by the hand, and tutored her in the manly art of puncture mending, as I think indeed I dared to say in the course of the review, perhaps hoping that one day many years hence, when we finally met in person, she would say: 'Miles Kington? Oh, you're the man who was going to show me how to mend a puncture! Well, it's never too late, is it?' Well, yes, I think it probably is. We still haven't met, and time is running out fast …

All of which shows that I had not grasped what the book was really all about. The whole point of *Life and Other Punctures* was not punctures, but life. Eleanor Bron was one of those people who cannot write about themselves or their own experiences unless they pretend they are writing about something else quite different. Put them in front of a screen or notebook and say 'Tell us all about your childhood,' and their minds go blank. Put them down in the same place and tell them to write about their recent trip to France, and you often find that their recent trip to France reminds them about something from their childhood and it all starts pouring out.

I can still remember a description by Eleanor Bron in the book of how she learnt to swim. It was in a pool in some exotic place where she was living as a child, or staying on a long holiday, a far-off exotic tropical place full of exotic flying insects, thousands of which had fluttered to their death in the pool, so that progress through the water was barred by masses of furry little bodies, all queuing up to try to get into Bron's mouth whenever it opened for breath, and her triumph at learning to swim was outweighed by the horror of trying not to swallow the insect world ... Grimly memorable, especially for a book about cycling in the North of France.

Some writers prefer to let their life details reappear in their novels. If you want to learn about me, said Jean Cocteau, don't look at my lying memoirs – look at my truthful novels. And he's right – that's what a writer's life is for – turning into fiction. What's the point of just writing it down as life? That's about as sensible as asking an actor to use his own real-life clothes on stage. Lots of writers do write their own life stories, of course, but only the boring ones write it down just as it happened, accurately, soberly and conscientiously; any writer worth his salt improves the story until it is worth telling. (As Eric Ambler must have been thinking when he entitled his book of memoirs *Here Lies Eric Ambler*.)

The moral is that if Eleanor Bron was good at mending punctures, we might have had a nice little book about pedalling through Normandy, but because she wasn't, we got a wonderful little self-portrait.

Gill, I know what you are going to say.

I know what you are going to say, because I am going to say it as well.

If Bron gave us a wonderful little self-portrait, how come it is out of print, totally unknown and quite forgotten?

It's a good point.

And the fact that if people buy *A Hundred Things to Do Before You Die*, by Miles Kington, and delightedly learn how to master punctures, then they will never write books like Eleanor Bron's, does tend to undermine my point even further.

So what is my point?

My point is that Patty Schultz's book *1,000 Places to See Before You Die* (A No. 1 *NY Times* Bestseller, God bless it) is not actually going to get the readers rushing off to Ayers Rock and Notre Dame, which is probably a good thing as far too many go there already. What it is going to do is leave those readers feeling strangely unsatisfied and unfulfilled because whereas before reading the book they knew there were a good few places they really ought to go and see one day, now they know there are at least a thousand places they should move heaven and earth to see, and they *know* they won't do it, and they might as well die now, because they are obviously feeble and unworthy ... Yes, reading Schultz's book is going to leave them profoundly unhappy.

Whereas reading *A Hundred Things to Do Before You Die*, by Miles Kington, will present every reader with at least two or three things they always meant to do and which they can now do *without leaving home or even spending any money*.

Here are some more of my hundred things to learn to do.

'Learn to Throw a Frisbee Properly at Last.'
'How to Take Your First Steps in Juggling.'
'Get – and Keep – that Space on the Beach or by the Pool.'
'Learn How to Tell the Difference Between a Planet and a Star.'
'Strokes and Heart Attacks – a Spotter's Guide – or, Why That Chap Over There Is Having a Hard Time.'
'How to Skip with a Skipping Rope so Economically, Stylishly and Smoothly that it Hardly Qualifies as Exercise at All.'
'How to Make Children at Adjacent Tables Burst into Tears for No Apparent Reason.'
'Keeping your Family Tree Safe from Blight and

Honey Fungus Through the Long Winter
    Months.'
'It's Never Too Late to Learn How to Shoplift.'
'Mastering Survival Techniques Equally Suitable for
    Broken Down Lifts, Abandoned Trains and
    Standing in a Security Queue in Heathrow
    Airport.'
'Beating a Duvet at its Own Game.'
'Learning Bar Billiards from Scratch.'

Well, Gill, I think you get the idea.

What do you think of *A Hundred Things to Do Before You Die*, by Miles Kington?

And if the answer is that you are going to look very seriously into the idea of reissuing Eleanor Bron's *Life and Other Punctures*, then I shall be very disappointed.

Love,
Miles

Blackmail

Dear Gill,

I have just had a thought about the book outlined in my previous letter.

What about a small change to the title?

Instead of calling it *A Hundred Things to Do Before You Die* by Miles Kington, what about it calling it *A Hundred Things to Do Before I Die* by Miles Kington?

Thus introducing an element of blackmail into the whole business.

If Patty Schultz can do it, so can I.

Just a thought.

Love,
Miles

Canal Bench

Dear Gill,

On the Kennet and Avon Canal near where I live, at occasional intervals along the picturesque towpath, there is the odd bench to sit on. Not generally provided by British Waterways, but by relatives who wanted to provide a memorial to their late departed loved one. You know that, because they generally have engraved brass plates on them. 'TO ALAN BROWN, WHO LOVED THIS CANAL', 'IN MEMORY OF ALAN BROWN, WHO LOVED THIS PARTICULAR SPOT'. Or even, in one uninspired case, 'TO ALAN BROWN'.

These benches are quite useful. I have often myself used them as a place to do up my shoes on, or to sit on and write notes of stuff going round in my head during a bike ride. I have often found that the mind goes into free wheel more easily on a bike ride than anywhere else in the world, and you get some really good thoughts up there on the saddle. Indeed, some of the ideas in these letters first saw the light of scribble on one of those benches.

So, if there is any money accruing from any of the books which I may have written as a consequence of any of these letters which I have written to you, between now and my death, I would like you to arrange for a bench to be bought and dedicated to me along the canal.

And I would like the following wording to be carved on the bench, or, better, put on that small plaque:

'IN FOND MEMORY OF MILES KINGTON, WHO HATED THIS SPOT, BECAUSE THERE WAS NEVER ANYWHERE TO SIT DOWN AND ENJOY IT FROM'

It doesn't matter where you put the bench, as long as there isn't one there already.

I'm afraid this isn't an idea for a book, only an idea on how to spend the royalties. Oh, well.

Love,
Miles

Cobblers and Cleft Palates

Dear Gill,

When you've got cancer, and you feel it entitles you to start sentences with the rather flashy words 'When you've got cancer', it must be extremely irritating for all those other people who have not got cancer to hear us say, 'When you have got cancer', as if it automatically makes us wiser or morally superior or more experienced in life or more dignified, whereas we are nothing of the sort. Just a bit more ill.

Still, when you have got cancer, you do notice one or two little odd things which other people don't, one of which is the sudden proliferation round the house of things like skewers and knitting needles and cork-screws, sometimes covered in blood, sometimes not.

Do you know why?

(Please say No.)

Since you don't know why, I'll tell you.

It's because you've been trying to pierce new holes in your old belts.

If you're a man, of course. And a woman, too, because women wear belts as well.

The thing is that when you get cancer you start to lose weight. You do not only lose weight, you lose inches round the waist. It's the sort of thing that you always prayed would happen to you, until it actually starts happening to you.

In my trim days, my waist was a good, elegant 32", but when I started to enjoy food more and take less exercise, in my fifties, it gradually crept up to 36", nudging 37". It never got any worse than that, but I always hoped that it would reverse the trend. And now it has, and I am down to 31", 32", again. However, it is not a slim, elegant 32" any more; it is a scrawny, puckered-navel kind of thinness, which means among other things that having tightened all my belts progressively, I have now come to the last hole provided and beyond. I now have to make new holes in my belt to accommodate the new thin me, so that I can pull the belt tight and insert the whatsit in the hole. (What is that thing called? That little metal spike on a belt?*)

Making a new hole is easier said than done. My belts seem to be made on the whole of rather good-quality leather, resistant to invasive surgery. I myself am not as strong as I used to be. So when I get a

---

* It's a prong. Obvious, really, once you know. (Ed.)

corkscrew or skewer and start excavating where the new hole should be, I tend to make more of a tiny dent than a hole. The more I fail, the more desperately I try. Hence the abandoned tools all over the place. And the blood marks.

The simplest thing to do would be to swallow my pride and take all my belts down to the local cobbler, explain the situation and get him to punch the extra holes. All cobblers have the necessary device for this. I once bought a belt in the small Irish town of Bantry, from an old-fashioned cobbler's, and when I asked the cobbler to punch an extra hole, he produced this macho ticket puncher with different calibre bits, which revolved until he found the right bit, and inserted my belt and attempted to punch a hole. In fact, he was older then than I am now, and found it very difficult even with his gadget to make a hole in the leather. I remember clenching and unclenching my muscular fists like a young god, and saying: 'Shall I have a go, then?', to which there was no answer from him, only a whisper in my ear from my companion: 'Never offer to help an Irish cobbler. It's a matter of pride,' which is a piece of advice I have never forgotten, or indeed used …

Most cobblers don't call themselves 'cobblers' any more, of course. They call themselves 'Heelbars', because mostly what they are called upon to do is instant resoling and reheeling of ladies' shoes, whereas the name 'cobbler' probably has too many clumsy overtones for the ladies. There are two cobbler's shops near where I live. One, in the city of Bath, is urban and calls itself a Heelbar. The other is much more rural, in Bradford on Avon, where it sits on a suicidal roundabout and calls itself a Cobbler's.

For that reason alone I think I would rather go to the Bradford on Avon set-up. Not because it is suicidal, though I often wonder how any of us ever get to the front door along a pavement six inches wide with lorries thundering past, but because it is happy to be called a Cobbler's. It feels like a cobbler's. It smells like a cobbler's. The Heelbar in Bath, which is terribly efficient, no question, smells of hot metal and hurry, but the Cobbler's in Bradford on Avon is full of nice old wooden shelves carrying old blank keys and shoe laces past their tie-by date, and it smells of old leather. The cobbler does lots of things beside soles and heels. He copies almost every kind of key it's legal to copy. He sells dog tags and inscribes the dog's name on them for you. He sells laces, polish and shoe cream of colours you didn't think shoes could come in. He sells and inscribes tankards. He punches holes in belts. He has a retractable walking stick and dogs' leads.

He also has a bad case of a cleft palate. It is almost impossible to make out what he is saying, as he makes no concession to it whatsoever, and talks to you as if he were clearly comprehensible, leaving you to pick up the meaning.

It's all right when *you* are doing the talking. You can make him understand everything you are saying, as indeed why shouldn't he? So you say, very clearly: 'I need a name tag for a dog, please, and a spare,' or: 'Can you copy this key for me?' and he says: 'Ang cha ang cha ang cha ang cha?' and you haven't the faintest idea what *he* is saying. Panic. You don't want to offend him. At the same time you don't want to end up with a blank dog tag, or a car key with 'Shep' stamped on it, so you try to work out what he might be asking you, and the only safe thing to do in that case, really, is to frame an answer which covers all possible angles, as in:

'Well, I'll be needing two of them please, and the name of the dog is written down on this bit of paper, together with our phone number, and any colour is fine, and my name is Kington, K-I-N-G-T-O-N, and I'm happy to pay in advance if that's what you want and come back to collect later …'

And he looks at you very patiently and says: 'Ang cha ang cha ang cha ang cha chen minnit OK?' And you are just about to give up and say, Forget it, I'll go to the place in Bath, when you suddenly pick up on the 'chen minnit' and you realise in a flash of intuition that he is saying 'Ready in ten minutes, OK?'

You say: 'Ready in ten minutes?'

49

He says: 'Chen minnit, OK?'

You burble, in sheer relief: 'Well, I've just got a bit of shopping to do, bookshop, chemist, Karen's for fruit and veg, so I'll be back in maybe a quarter of an hour, oh, and perhaps the Post Office too …'

And he nods and you nod. And off you go, because it's almost all finished now, all except the eventual discussion of how much it costs ('ang cha ang cha ang cha ang cha 50p …') over which we will draw a veil.

Recently the cobbler with the cleft palate has acquired a colleague who is very cheery and speaks normally, which is a relief in a way, except that of course you are naturally drawn to talk to the new guy because you can understand everything he says back, and it does occur to me that if *everyone* now ignores the old bloke with the cleft palate, then he may well harbour a huge resentment against the new guy, which will lead to some kind of terrible power struggle, especially when the old guy tries to win back his share of the conversation and the new guy naturally tries to intercede every time he senses the old guy is not making himself understood …

A cobbler's shop would not be a good place for a power struggle to break out, or, to put it another way, it would be a very good place for it. There isn't much room in there, and it's full of knives and awls and adzes and power machines and grinders, so that if ever the situation erupted in violence or a physical tussle, I for one would not want to get the worst of it and wake up with a ring through my nose or the name 'Shep' stamped on my forehead …

Gill, I cannot now remember what idea for a book I was going to suggest when I started this letter, and all that seems to have come of it is an idea for a violent denouement in a cobbler's shop, which is not my kind of thing at all, so I suggest you ignore it and we move on.

Love,
Miles

PS I was talking to Caroline, my wife, about the cobbler's shop in Bradford, and it seems I have misread the situation. The new guy is not a colleague. He has actually bought the shop as a going concern. But the old guy refuses to stop coming to work. It is the only place he knows. The new guy is desperate for him to stop coming, but doesn't know how to arrange it, without pushing him over the edge.

Perhaps my fears of a violent denouement are not so far-fetched after all …

Weight Loss – 1

Dear Gill,

The first thing I noticed about all this business was losing weight. I don't mean that I noticed I was losing weight and thought: 'Aha – I'm losing weight! I must have cancer!' I just noticed that I was losing weight. (If I had thought about it at all, I might have started wondering *why* I was losing weight, because there is always a reason for those things, but like many people I thought it was just something that was happening.)

So there you have it. Weight Loss Through Cancer. Thousands of people are desperate to lose weight. Desperate. Some of them might be desperate enough to think seriously of losing weight through cancer …

Love,
Miles

Weight Loss – 2

Dear Gill,

I have just reread my last letter and thought 'What a load of rubbish.'

Nobody is that desperate.

Not even Luciano Pavarotti.

He died of the same kind of cancer as I have got, you know, and he also had a weight problem. What I would like to know is if his gross obesity fell away towards the end of his life.

Because if it did, I see a space for a book called *The Luciano Pavarotti Way to Weight Loss*.

I don't know what would be in it, but I think it's a good idea for a title.

Love,
Miles

Cancer – IFAQs

Dear Gill,

I have noticed that when people get any kind of illness these days, they go on to the Internet to research it, or they go out and buy a book about it, or, judging from my Amazon-fixated friends, they combine the two by going on the Internet to buy a book about it. I am much more in favour of them buying a book, as I have no idea how to make money out of the Internet, but I can't see me writing an introductory book to the basic facts about cancer. Can you imagine it? *The Do's and Don'ts of Cancer*, or *An Introduction to Cancer*, or, as they would say these days, *Cancer – the FAQs* by Dr Miles Kington. I don't see it. It's not my bag.

But I do see an area which I could explore, and which I suspect has not been opened up yet, and that is the odd hinterland of cancer which has been totally ignored in the rush to make things scientific and simple and unscary.

Cancer – the IFAQs.

Cancer – the infrequently asked questions.

The things about cancer that nobody tells you, because you've never asked and they wouldn't know the answer anyway.

Questions like these:

1.   Who is the patron saint of cancer?
2.   Can the experience of dying of cancer be offered as part of the Duke of Edinburgh's Award Scheme?
3.   Who was the first person to dare to use the word 'cancer' on radio or TV? (Kenneth Tynan? Johnny Rotten? Dr Anthony Clare?)
4.   If your spouse dies of cancer, can you offload the penalty points from your driving licence on to his or her unexpired driving licence, and then start again with a clean sheet?
5.   It is well known that George VI died of cancer, but was there any link between that and his lifelong hobby of philately?
6.   That is, is there any connection between the licking of stamps and stamp hinges, and the contraction of cancer?
7.   Has any research been done into this?
8.   Why not?
9.   Did the king actually lick his own stamp hinges, or was there a Philatelist Royal who did it for him?

10. If so, is there any record of whether the man who licked the stamp hinges for George got cancer or not?

11. Why not?

You see what I am driving at, Gill. The lateral approach to cancer. They may not be questions which everyone with cancer wants to ask, but you cannot deny that you wanted to know the answers, can you?

Here are some more questions about cancer.

12. What does it mean to be in denial about cancer?

13. We all think we know what it means to be in denial, that is, to flagrantly ignore the cold facts, but how can you be in denial over cancer?

14. If you're told you've got cancer, how can you deny it, apart from demanding a second opinion?

15. If the second opinion says you've got cancer, how long do you go on disbelieving all the tests and experts?

16. Or does it mean that although deep down you know you've got cancer, you would rather not think about it?

17. Which, actually, is not so much denial, is it, as just cold-shouldering?

18. And there again, if you are one of those cheery customers who have been told you have got cancer but who prefer to carry on regardless, is that denial?

19. Or reckless bravery?

20. And if you are one of those tough cookies who say, Dammit! I can be cured! I will recover! I am not going to lie down and give in! – What then? Is that denial? Or is it denial of denial?

21. And if you pursue all other kinds of alternative treatment, in search of a cure, are you in denial of the plain statistic that most people will *not* be cured by alternative treatment?

22. Are optimism and hopefulness only disguised forms of denial?

23. Will I just shut up about denial for a moment?

24. Don't you realise that hopeful and optimistic questions about denial can be very depressing?

25. Isn't there some other question which is infrequently asked?

26. Yes. One question which rarely occurs to a cancer patient to ask is: Can other animals besides humans get cancer?

27. Yes. We know or at least vets know that dogs and cats and cows get what seems to be cancer. (There is also a theory that wasps and bees can get cancer, which is why they sometimes seem extremely bad-tempered and vicious, even when you think you are being nice to them. Luckily, wasps and bees with cancer are mostly too feeble to sting you.)

28. Can animals with cancer be cured?

29. Mmm – tough one, this. Orthodox treatment sometimes seems to work, but it is hard to tell whether they benefit from alternative treatment. Much of the effect of alternative treatment depends on a) you *knowing* that it is alternative; and b) you paying a lot of money for it, both of which are beyond the understanding of animals. So it's a slightly vexed question.

30. Excuse me, but what is a vexed question? I can see how people can be vexed or annoyed, but how can a *question* be vexed? I've always thought that a question had a certain calmness and self-confidence. It's answers, if anything, that would have to do the worrying. Questions have lots of self-confidence. Answers don't. Isn't it much more likely to be a vexed answer, than a question?

31. Oh, for heaven's sake! Couldn't we just have questions about cancer, please?

32. All right. Do people born under the sign of Cancer actually suffer more from cancer than people under other signs?

33. No.

34. No?

35. Less, actually.

36. Really?

37. Yes.

38. How come?
39. Well, if you examine the death rates of all the twelve Zodiac signs, you are bound to find that *one* of them has the highest cancer rate. One of them must. It's like finding that one month has the highest road death rate, or one season has the most sunshine. So one sign is bound to have the most cancer cases. It happens to be Aquarius, actually. But there again, there also has to be a star sign with the most heart attacks, or suicides, etc.
40. And?
41. And what?
42. And which signs have the most heart attacks, suicides, etc.?
43. Aquarius.
44. What, ALL of them?
45. Yes. Heart attacks, cancer, suicides, everything.
46. But that's incredible! How is it possible that in every single case … ?

AN AQUARIOLOGIST WRITES:

Hello! Let me introduce myself. I am an Aquariologist. That is to say, I am an astrologer who specialises in the particular problems and properties peculiar to those who were born under the sign of Aquarius.

You probably never realised that some

astrologers were restricted to one sign. Most people believe that every astrologer deals equally with all Zodiac signs. But a moment's thought will reveal how unlikely this is. Does one doctor deal with all known diseases? Can one instructor teach you to play all sports? Would you really want to learn golf from a cricketing coach?

Similarly, you can see what good sense it makes to have one astrologer looking after one sign. Don't forget that even an astrologer is born under a particular sign! Therefore, like most Aquarians, there are certain signs I am not drawn towards, such as Taurus and Capricorn, and even one sign which I feel distinctly hostile towards. (No names, no pack drill!)

So what happens if, as an astrologer, I am consulted by one of these opposing sign-holders? Exactly! I will have to fight to remain neutral. I will have to ignore my own feelings. Not easy. So I made the momentous decision eventually that I would cater only for people born in Aquarius, people I can relate to, people who know they can relate to me.

Of course, when I say 'only people born in Aquarius', that is still a huge amount of people! One twelfth of the world population! We Aquarians are as numerous as the others (I have checked this) and therefore by specialising in one sign I am not exactly endangering my livelihood. Are you surprised when a garage says it will service and repair only Saab cars? I don't think so. And yet there are more Aquarians than Saab cars! It makes sense.

Q: I am with you so far. But you haven't answered the big question yet.

Aquariologist: Which big question?

Q: Do Aquarians, statistically, die more often, or younger, of cancer than people born under other signs?

Aquariologist: If you care to make an appointment to see me, I am quite happy to talk about this to you, for the appropriate fee. This is not something I care to talk about casually.

Q: I do not see how I can make an appointment to see you, I am a Taurean.

Aquariologist: Then go see a Taurologist!

Q: OK, OK. But before I go, can you just have a look at my Saab 900? It sometimes makes a strange burning smell in the engine ...

Aquariologist: No problem ... let me just see the log book ... Ah, here we are ... manufactured 1991, fourth month, third week ... so, this car would have come off the assembly line in Sweden when Uranus was in conjunction with Mars, moving into the influence of Venus ... oh dear, it's beginning to look like an oil problem, isn't it?

CANCER: Infrequently Asked Questions
A New Handbook for the Open Mind
By Dr Miles Kington

(Doctor Kington has professional qualifications which can always be viewed in his premises in a big glass frame over the fireplace, from The Mail Order Degree of Medicine Service, San Jacinto Collegiate Foundation, Texas, 24-Hour Service, No Subject Too Obscure.)

I think I may have got too close to this one, Gill. Can you see any future in it?

Love,
Miles

Patron Saint

Dear Gill,

Is there a patron saint of cancer?
St Rita?*

Love,
Miles

---

* Patron saint of lost causes. (Ed.)

Clearing Out My Papers Prior to My Death

Dear Gill,

The best time to joke about death is when you think you're never going to die. When he was young and gay, Woody Allen wrote a wonderful, very funny play about death called *Death*. In his earlier pieces he sometimes introduced Death as a character, either young and inexperienced or elderly and Jewish and hopeless. Now that Woody Allen is older and balder, I don't notice him doing so many gags about Death. (In fact, I don't notice him doing many gags at all about anything.) And I would be prepared to bet that when Ingmar Bergman did his famous scenes with Death in *The Seventh Seal*, he was not an old man. (I've just looked it up. In his late thirties. Young enough.)

When I was writing my intended bestseller, *Someone Like Me*, I invented a mother who often retired in the mid-afternoon to go to bed to die, or to have a death-bed scene, which I am not sure I would have enjoyed writing so much now that my death is closer than it used to be.

Similarly, there was a time when I used to start letters, usually in very belated reply to someone, as follows: 'Dear so-and-so, While sorting out my papers prior to my death, I came across a letter from you which …'

And if I felt there was an explanation necessary for this attention-seeking opening, I would go on to add this:

'What I mean by this is that my papers are in some disarray. Some considerable disarray. It has taken me twenty years at least to create this devolution into potential chaos. Assuming the mess gets cleared up at the same rate at which it is created, I reckon it will therefore take me another twenty years to get everything straight, which gives me a good twenty years before I die. So, when I say "prior to my death", this is not as ominous as it sounds …'

Considering that I have been uttering this formula for what seems like a dozen years at least, you might say that I am well on the way to achieving that twenty years before I die, which is quite good.

What is not so good is that my papers really do need clearing up prior to my death. I may have been making that joke for a long time, but I have not been clearing up my papers in real life to keep pace with the joke.

Well, you know what it's like.

It all starts one day when you set off to find out what your National Insurance number is, because your accountant says you will go to prison if you don't find it.

You know where it is. It is in a file marked 'Personal Details'. Or 'Finance'. Or 'Household Expenses' or even 'That National Insurance Number You've Been Looking For Everywhere'.

And as you are looking for that file, you come across another one called 'Barcelona 1999', which is full of receipts from the first visit to Barcelona you ever made, organised by your wife as a birthday present. It was a great weekend, but do you really need a folder containing the details of a trip to Catalonia nearly ten years ago? Shouldn't you just chuck the whole thing out, instead of allowing it to accumulate with so many other folders?

Yes, of course, is the answer.

But you don't chuck it out.

It was a lovely weekend and even the receipts have a poetic aftertaste.

So you put it back in the pile of folders.

And you are glad you didn't chuck it out, because hardly five years later, you find you are booked in again to go to Barcelona prior to a long train trip to Murcia, which actually happened to me in 2007, and your wife says: 'I'd love to go back to that restaurant we went to in Barcelona last time we were there – do you remember what it was called?' Which also happened to me.

And you say, with a surge of excitement, 'No, but I know where I can lay my hands on it!' and you go off to dig out that Barcelona folder and it has completely vanished. It has gone to ground. It has hibernated. It has been recycled. On the other hand, you do find – no, not your National Insurance number, life is never that neat – you do find a folder you had never noticed before labelled 'Ideas for Articles', and as you are currently short of ideas for articles, and indeed chronically short, you look eagerly inside. There is nothing in there. This suggests strongly either a) that you never had any ideas, or b) you had some and used them all up. Still, at least you can relax safe in the knowledge that if you ever come to have any unused ideas for articles in the future, you now have somewhere to put them. If you can find that folder next time round.

I think there is a TV programme here.

It has become quite fashionable to make TV programmes about clearing up, clearing out, sorting your possessions, sorting other people's stuff out, getting rid of clothes that don't suit you. Changing, rethinking, reinventing, decluttering ...

But nobody has done a programme, I think, about putting your life in order with a view to giving you an easier death.

Oh yes, they have done close-up, in-your-face documentaries on fatal diseases and how they affect families, marriages and loved ones. There have been intimate portraits of people facing up to their last moments on earth, and facing up to the great void beyond.

Forget the great void.

What about the great mess?

What about facing twenty years of accumulation, the piles of papers, the overflowing documents on the desk, and indeed on the carpet round the desk?

There's a programme there, surely?

'Miles Kington Clears His Desk and Dies'.

'Prior to His Death – Miles Kington's Last Clear-Up.'

'Sorting Out My Papers Prior to My Death – Miles Kington Looks for His National Insurance Number.'

Or, if the worst comes to the worst:

'Lunch in Barcelona for One.'

I don't think the title is quite right yet, but that's a detail. If you can sell the programme idea, I am sure the title will follow. As luck would have it, I do actually have a folder labelled 'Great Ideas for Titles for Good TV Programmes'. Next time I see it, I'll have a look inside and report back to you.

Love,
Miles

PART II

Crossing the Plateau

The Power of Self-Pity

Dear Gill,

People are making a lot of money out of self-help books these days, and I would like you to be one of those people.

By helping to promote my new self-help book.

Which would be about self-pity.

Did you notice in my first letter that I referred to the jumble of self-pitying thoughts I first had when I was diagnosed with cancer?

My immediate response was to be apologetic for this stance, because we are always taught not to be sorry for ourselves, as if there were something dreadfully feeble about it. There are no nice words in English at all for 'self-pity'. There are lots of disapproving ones. Whingeing, sulking, moping, etc., etc.

(Personally, I think we are entitled to indulge in a little self-pity when we are told we have cancer, as long as we disguise it as something else. Shock, a nervous breakdown, long sobbing fits. Something like that.)

But self-pity is so common that it earns no respect at all, only disapproval, as in phrases like: 'Sitting around all day feeling sorry for herself,' or 'You'd think he was the only one who had ever had leukaemia.' Which quickly leads to phrases like: 'Why doesn't she just pull herself together?' and 'Cheer up, dear – it's only bi-polar disorder!'

My brilliant idea would be to turn it all round and treat self-pity as a potentially positive force.

It's certainly a very strong force.

It doesn't have to involve cancer. It need only be a cold. Especially if it's a man involved. Close up to a sufferer, you can feel the concentrated power of how sorry people, especially men, feel for themselves. What needs to be done is to turn that power into a positive force!

'The Positive Power of Self-Pity'

'How Whingeing Can Work For You!'

'Release the Grumble Factor!'

One of the nurses in the chemotherapy unit said to me the other day that it was very important to listen to your body, as very often your body knew instinctively what was good for it.

I told her that I often had a quick word with my body, looking for advice, and it was not unknown for my body to say: 'Poor old you!'

She was not impressed.

Like all medically trained people, she wanted the body to be more specific, and to offer clear-cut instructions.

Well, I told her, sometimes it told me to go upstairs and lie down and have a rest.

'Excellent!' she said. 'So have a rest!'

I didn't tell her that what my body actually says to me is: 'You poor old thing! Nobody really under-stands, do they? You go and have a lie-down right now. And I am really REALLY sorry I am causing you all this bother …'

Of course, if self-pity is left undeveloped and untreated, it can go slightly poisonous and feed on itself. (That doesn't really mean anything. It's the sort of thing that people write in self-help books. I am just practising so that I can write my own self-help book.)

It's not difficult to recognise the danger signs – the sufferer starts to enjoy his self-pity and will dom-inate the conversation, talking endlessly about his blood tests and wobbly veins, about platelets, lymph nodes and metastasis. However sympathetic at first, his audience will eventually lose patience. What he should be doing is converting that dead weight of self-pity into positive power …

'Brood Your Way Back to Health'

'Tap the Inner Energy of Apathy'

73

'There For The Taking – The Hidden Power of Hypochondria'

I definitely think there is a book there.

I would go into a little more detail except I haven't actually been feeling that good today.

I didn't sleep well last night, for a start, and the chap across the road has been using a strimmer all morning, which really gets on my nerves.

And as if that weren't bad enough …

I bet you've switched off already, haven't you, Gill?

That's because I've gone into self-pity mode.

Old self-pity mode.

But now I can see how to convert that useless sulking into positive power and action!

Already today, for example, I have sent my agent an idea for a bestseller, telling people how to convert crude self-pity into refined personal energy!

Yes – it really works!

Tell me what you think.

Love,
Miles

Cancer – Who to Trust?

Dear Gill,

Everyone knows a bit about cancer, I've discovered. Not much. But enough. Enough to talk a bit about it. Usually it takes the form of someone they knew who got cancer out of the blue, and all they know about cancer is based on their story.

That story comes in one of three or four forms.

1. The person they knew refused to give up. They said: 'I am not going to let this defeat me! It's me against cancer! But cancer does not always win, and it's not going to beat me!'

    And triumphantly for up to a year they survive, then die, probably exhausted by the overuse of all those exclamation marks.

2. The person they knew who suffered from cancer decided that whatever treatment they were getting, some other treatment might be better. So if they had landed among the NHS mob, and were getting some form of

chemotherapy or radiotherapy, they would become convinced that alternative treatment would be better, and would switch to the shadowy brotherhood of the smiley world of background music and expensive premises in the nice part of town, looking out over restfully manicured gardens which, it takes only a second to work out, has been paid for by your predecessors on the couch.

This person signs up wholeheartedly to the alternative gospel, but has usually died within a year, often tired out by the sheer tranquillity of those damned gardens. (Which, if they were to have any effect at all, should not be peaceful, but full of leaves and branches needing to be swept up into a bonfire. The garden should in fact be not some kind of visual therapy but a test. The patient should look out of the sash window and say: 'That needs clearing up! I can't sit here nattering about the will to live and reciprocal diets while that garden needs attention! Give me a garden fork, a pair of tough gloves and a box of matches, and I'll be back in an hour!' leaving the baffled alternative practitioner either feeling out of control or planning a new leaflet on *Cancer: A Cure in the Garden*.)

3.   The person they knew did their treatment and

got well again, which was so unexpected that they then went into a decline and gradually faded away.

4. The person they knew who suffered from cancer turns out to have been their husband or wife, and they nursed them and cared for them through their long, perhaps painful, illness, but they died anyway, and now they miss them dreadfully. Still. Years later. For ever and ever. Mavis Nicholson has never got over the death of Geoff Nicholson, Katharine Whitehorn is still desperate over Gavin Lyall's failure to survive. My wife, Caroline, is going to be distraught when I die. More than distraught, she is going to be furious. Already there is a vague undercurrent of feeling that I will be very unfair if I die, after all the trouble she has lavished on keeping me well-fed and ticking over nicely.

5. The person they knew who had been diagnosed with cancer turned out not to have had cancer at all. They had something else instead. Which killed them anyway. This person usually turns out to be Geoffrey Dickinson.

Love,
Miles

Geoffrey Dickinson – 1

Dear Gill,

Who was Geoffrey Dickinson?

Late last year I got a phone call from Bill Davis, who had been editor of *Punch* for most of the time I worked for that legendary humorous magazine. His predecessor was one of the old school called Bernard Hollowood (who unusually did both cartoons and articles, and neither very well), and afterwards Bill Davis left to make lots of money from running the British Airways in-flight magazine *High Life*.

Everyone on the staff of *Punch* under Bill Davis took against him, and we were all wrong. Bill saw us as a self-serving clique who used *Punch* as a private club to get our stuff printed, our old-fashioned, history-drenched, traditional little essays and bits of light verse, and he was right. I remember once hearing him storm down the *Punch* corridor (his office at one end, the library at the other) shouting: 'The trouble with this magazine is that it's too damned *literary*! I hate fine writing! I want funny writing!'

I was shocked. I had never heard 'literary' being used as an insult before. But Bill had not been to university and had not been brainwashed as we had. He wasn't even English. He was born German, and his mother brought him over to London after the war when she left his father and got hitched to a British soldier. Can you imagine what it was like for a young German lad to land in East London in 1946 and have to make a new life? Twenty years later, in the 1960s, we didn't make it easy for him and although by then you couldn't tell he had ever been German, except when he called a 'folk song' a 'volk song', or pronounced Michael ffolkes as 'Michael Volks', we still refused to make it easy for him.

Yet he breezed through it all, because, I now realise, he was nicer than all of us put together, and he never let it get to him. He rose above it. He let us have our playground rituals, our fun and games at his expense, and by the time he had done his stint at *Punch* he was ready to move on to a more prosperous life and we were still hack humorists who hadn't the faintest idea where to go next.

And then I got this phone call from him. He sounded bright and cheerful. He always sounded bright and cheerful. He sounded as if he was delighted to hear my voice. (Do you know? I think he liked me. When I think of all the spiteful things I may have thought and said about him over the years, I feel quite ashamed, especially as he repaid it with true affection. Sorry, Bill. They were good days.)

'Miles!' he said. 'Long time no see! How are you?'

'Not well.' I said. Sometimes I plunge straight to the cancer story. Mostly I don't. With Bill, I felt it was right. 'Actually I have been diagnosed with cancer.'

'Oh, no! Not you, too!' he wailed.

It's not often you can accurately say that someone has *wailed*, but that's what it sounded like.

'What do you mean, "you too"?' I said.

'Well, I rang you to find out if you knew that Alan was on his last legs with cancer. I was going to let you gently in on it …'

'Yes, I know.'

I knew because the obituary department of the *Independent* had already rung me, saying he was not expected to live long, and could I do a piece on him. I told Bill I was already working on his obituary, in advance, and he sighed.

'Now, don't forget Geoffrey Dickinson,' he said. 'Anyone who thinks he has got cancer should remember Geoffrey Dickinson. Get a second opinion! Now!'

Geoff was my best mate at *Punch*. He was the assistant art editor. He was a bluff, sensitive, talented, hard-drinking lad from Formby in Lancashire who decided to forgive my public school background and give me a chance to redeem myself, sensing that there was still good in me. Occasionally he and I went on overseas *Punch* trips together, me doing the words, him the drawings. Spain, we got to. Brussels, to report on the extraordinary European School for the elitist children of elitist Eurocrats. The farthest we ever got was Goa and Bombay …

After he left *Punch*, Geoff was diagnosed with some form of liver cancer and told he could never drink again. Agonisingly, he gave up the booze. After six years he was told they had got it wrong, and it was safe for him to drink. Several months later, he was dead, of whatever was REALLY wrong with him, which they never established fully.

'They were wrong with Geoffrey!' said Bill. 'They might be wrong with you! Get a second opinion! Geoffrey could have had six happy drinking years, and he missed them! Don't let it happen to you!'

'Okay, Bill,' I said humbly. It was quite like the old days. 'Meanwhile, I'd better get to work on Alan Coren.'

'I hadn't seen much of Alan recently,' said Bill. 'Our paths didn't cross a lot.'

'I hadn't seen him at all,' I said. 'I left *Punch* in 1980. Never seen him again, except at other people's memorial services, like Barry Took's.'

Bill Davis had already wailed, and sighed. Now he shrieked.

'But you and he were great mates! You and Alan!'
I thought about it.

'Bill, we were never even friends. I never went to his house and he never got invited to mine. We never ever mixed outside the office. We didn't even particularly like each other, I think.'

'And now he's lying there, dying of lung cancer,' said Bill, who didn't always listen to what you were saying. 'Did he smoke? I don't remember him smoking.'

One of the things that everyone remembers about Alan is that he smoked like a chimney. Chain smoked. Silk Cut, I think. Small, nasty filter cigarettes. Geoffrey Dickinson smoked too, I think. I know I did. We all did, then. Except for Bill Davis, who liked the occasional festive cigar, but nothing else to puff, so you must remind me to tell you of the time his father, over from Germany, turned to me and said, 'Ich möchte schließlich nicht, dass mein Sohn zum Kettenraucher wird!'

'So don't forget Geoffrey Dickinson,' said Bill. 'Get a second opinion. Keep drinking. Don't give up anything.'

I said goodbye to Bill and went off to write the obituary of Alan Coren.

Love,
Miles

Geoffrey Dickinson – 2

Dear Gill,

I loved Geoffrey Dickinson. But then everyone loved Geoffrey Dickinson. I never met anyone who disliked him. My wife Caroline, who I had met not long before he died, says she still remembers being staggered by the huge turn-out for his memorial service at St Bride's in Fleet Street. Yet he was not famous, not hugely talented, not a star. He could draw alright, and he and Bill Hewison (his art editor at *Punch*, while he was number two) made a very good art team who got *Punch* laid out every week and made it look good, and I still have quite a handful of his original drawings and painted covers, which are all quite nice and chunky, but I would swap them all for a single ffolkes or Heath Robinson. Or a Bill Hewison, come to that.

(I think maybe his art would have been better for being less nice and chunky. He himself was on the small side, and some cartoonists and illustrators

– like Anton – react to being diminutive in person by drawing their characters very tall and elegant, but he never did. He should have tried it.)

He came from Lancashire, from Formby, from a solid lower middle class background. He claimed to be mates with Beryl Bainbridge as kids. I think he went to grammar school, then trained at the Royal Academy. By coincidence, he was not the only person called Dickinson on the *Punch* staff. Out of a total of maybe a dozen, there were two Dickinsons, Geoffrey and the Hon. Peter Dickinson, who I hasten to say, never used his Hon. Peter was a very clever, attractive, intelligent, somewhat saintly man, who wrote screeds of light verse, and had been to some very posh public school. Winchester, it was. I remember this because one day in the office Peter and I were having a discussion about the different varieties of the game of fives. (Fives is an ancient kind of squash played with gloves, not rackets, in which you lam the handball as violently as you can against the far wall, then get out of the way as fast as possible for your opponent to do the same back again.)

Anyway, there are different kinds of fives called things like Eton Fives and Winchester Fives, all depending on the actual shape of the side wall of the court, and as Peter and I idly tried to work out which was which, Geoffrey happened to come past and started listening to our discussion. When it came to an end, he looked at me sorrowfully and said 'Oh, Miles, I thought you were one of us, but you're not, after all, are you? You're one of them.' Meaning, a public school monster who really thought that these things were important. I was dreadfully wounded, especially as, next to an Old Wykehamist like Peter, I wasn't a posh public school type at all, just an odd product of a Scottish boarding school which would never have anything named after it.

I had the public school trappings all right, but I didn't feel that my soul had been sold. I felt a lot closer to Geoffrey than to Peter. I think I spent part of the rest of my life trying to prove to Geoff that I *wasn't* one of them and indeed, although Geoff and I went away on trips together as often as we could, and got on famously, I could never imagine going on a trip anywhere with the Hon. Peter Dickinson, who was far too cool and patrician, whereas Geoff and I giggled and indulged in horseplay and mucked around the whole time.

Love,
Miles

Farewell to a Dog

Dear Gill,

I now realise that there is a strong possibility that my dog and cat might outlive me.

Less likely with the cat, who is fourteen and quite an old lady, even though she still behaves like a teenager. Only this morning she climbed on my lap while I was working, which was, as it always is, a) very sweet, and b) a bloody nuisance. She won't be around for much longer, I fear.

But our dog, Berry, is a healthy 10-year-old springer spaniel who has got at least another five years in him, probably more. I had always put to the back of my mind the thought of his final decline and death, which was bound to come when I was about seventy, especially if we finally had to have him put down.

Now, though, I see that I might be the first one to go, which puts things in a very different light.

He might not realise that I am going to die, for a

start. He doesn't know about death. As I lie expiring, surrounded by people who got tickets for the event in time, how do I know that as I open my mouth and prepare to utter my carefully prepared and rehearsed last words, he may not burst in and demand to be taken for a walk?

And that my last words, after all that, will turn out to be: 'Oh, for God's sake, not now, Berry!'

I have not mentioned him anywhere in my will, and yet I suppose he is a dependant of sorts. More than most, really. Should I not cater for him as well? If only to stop him asking me if I have got all my affairs sorted out?

' … To my dog Berry, who was the only one of my close ones NOT to ask if had got my affairs sorted out, I therefore in gratitude leave … Everything.'

Tempting.

And people seem to do well out of pet books.

What do you think, in my case?

How to Say Goodbye to a Dog.

(And How To Leave It All Your Money, If You Have To.)

It's an idea.

Tell me what you think.

Love,
Miles

Famous Last Words

Dear Gill,

Famous last words have rather gone out of fashion recently. All the famous famous last words were said by people who died a long time ago. Nobody has recently said anything memorable on their death-beds, and do you know why? It is because people don't have deathbeds any more.

Oh yes, they die in bed all right, but not in the old-fashioned way, surrounded by grieving or greedy relations, old friends, doctors and priests. The dying man or woman would be propped up on their pillow, and everyone while pretending to weep would be secretly waiting for the dying mouth to open and say something, which I guess is how we know that Goethe said 'More light!' and Pitt said 'I think I could eat one of Bellamy's veal pies,' the only example I know of product placement in dying words.

Dying words like those are pretty banal, but of course when they were uttered, the utterer didn't know they were going to be the last words he would ever utter. You can't hang on till you think of something more pithy and then lapse into intentional silence so that that remains your dying statement.

Nevertheless, some quite pithy last words have been recorded. People like to quote Heinrich Heine's 'Dieu me pardonnera – c'est son métier.' ('God will forgive me – it's his job', though I can't help feeling it sounds better in French. What would be a better translation? 'God will forgive me – that's what he's there for'? 'That's what he does' …) I wonder, if having said that, he then clammed up. Or if, after having requested his veal pie, Pitt was stricken with the desire to go out on a grander note and went before he could.

Oscar Wilde, famously, is remembered for two quite different exit lines. One is 'I shall die as I have lived – beyond my means.' The other is 'Either that wallpaper goes or I do!' Both quite good, certainly better than Goethe's poor old 'More light!', though even that has its distinction, as someone once pointed out that what he said in German ('Mehr Licht!') would have been exactly the same if he had been a Lowland Scot – 'Mair licht!'

My favourite dying words came from the Mexican revolutionary figure Pancho Villa, who lay dying in some flyblown corner of Mexico and found one of his men leaning over him ready to catch his parting words.

'Tell them,' said Pancho Villa, 'tell them that I said something interesting.'

Then he died.

Today, I am afraid, we all pass away cocooned in a final swaddling of drugs and painkillers and would find it impossible to utter any dying words even if we wanted to. As far as I can make out, the only people whose dying words are recorded these days are people who die in accidents or crashes or from sudden untimely death. Lady Diana, for instance, who said something like 'My God …' which is quite understandable if you've just hit a concrete pillar at over 100 mph.

Well, I have a small proposal to put all this right. I propose that we should all be able to register our final words in advance of our death. I propose that, once we have evolved and perfected our final statement, we should get over the difficulties of actually making it the last thing we physically say by setting up a simple, binding legal procedure to safeguard our final words, by ring-fencing them well in advance.

Love,
Miles

The Funeral Video – 1

Dear Gill,

Whenever I attend someone's memorial service, and there are witty, anecdotal, tearful, movingly comic speeches by the great and the good in memory of the late departed, I am always struck by one notable absence among the great and the good.

The late lamented himself.

Or herself.

Wouldn't it be great, I think, to have a short contribution from the person in whose honour we are all gathered, so that we could hear him once again telling one or two of his favourite stories, making caustic remarks about the other speakers and generally reminding us of why we all miss him so much?

Or her?

They do it at awards ceremonies. If someone gets a top award and can't be there for the actual ceremony, they very often manage to get the winner to do a brief video or film clip, shot on location in

Mozambique, lamenting their absence and often saying something wittier and more cogent than if they had been up on the podium in person.

So why can't they do it at memorial services? Or even at funerals? Instead of the clergyman who obviously never knew the late lamented, would it not be possible to have the lamented doing a brief last appearance instead?

For the last two or three years I have been daydreaming off and on about how I could contrive to be present at my own service.

The answer is quite simple.

Make a video in advance of my farewell speech, to be shown on a monitor from the pulpit, or on a screen behind the stage, or wherever the best place would be.

I have already visualised the opening shot.

It is of me, smiling ruefully, and saying to camera: 'Hello. I'm sorry I couldn't be here in person with you today …'

That much is definite. The rest of the script remains vague. I always swore I would get down to it one day, and I still haven't, which sums up the life of the freelance writer pretty well. 'When he died, he was still working on his farewell speech …'

I once touched on this idea when I was having lunch with Douglas Adams. I didn't know Douglas very well, but I liked him a lot. We were having an argument about gravestones, which he said were a waste of time and a useless Victorian survival, and should not be continued with.

I said they didn't have to be useless. It was merely the fault of the lazy masons and undertakers that they had never kept up with the times.

'What do you mean by that?' he said.

'Well,' I said, 'gravestones still give out the same ludicrously rudimentary information that they did two hundred years ago. Date of birth. Date of death. First names. Names of loved ones left behind. A pious message, perhaps. That was it. Obituaries have moved on. It's about time headstones did.'

'Yes, but how … ?'

'Easy,' I said. 'What you should install in a headstone is a small screen and a ten-minute video of the guy's life. The stone itself gives the basic details, but if you want more than that, you push the little button which says "Press Here For Life Highlights", and the screen lights up and you find yourself watching a ten-minute résumé of the man's life. Maybe it wouldn't be free. Maybe you would have to put a £1 coin in, to go towards grave upkeep.'

Douglas thought this would be a very good idea, and that it might even give a new meaning to the word 'grave-robber', meaning someone who broke into an ObitView device and took the cash.

ObitView? Gravestone News? AdieuView? Well,

whatever the name, I can see a fortune waiting to be made from the idea, and whoever makes it, it won't be me, and it won't be Douglas.

I wonder, as a matter of interest, how Douglas finally decided he himself wanted to be memorialised, and what sort of memorial stone guards his resting place. And what it says on it.

You have got more time than I have to find out, Gill, and better contacts too.

Love,
Miles

The Funeral Video – 2

Dear Gill,

My idea for a funeral video was not exactly an idea for a book, was it? Nor much of a money-maker either, if it is to be shown free at my service. I suppose it might attract broadcast fees if anyone wanted to show it, though I get the impression that any good short film clips get posted on websites called things like Facebook or U-Bend these days, where everyone can view them for free.

In any case, you and I have never talked much about performing, as my TV career came to an abrupt end when I turned down the chance to present *Around the World in Eighty Days* and thus gave Michael Palin his chance to come back from the dead and spend the rest of his life going on public transport in the Third World. Every now and then I get despairing emails from Michael somewhere in the Hindu Kush or the forests of Poland, saying: 'Miles – help – please come and take over from me – cannot stand this aimless life,' but I think he should have thought of that long ago, and I leave them unanswered.

Which means that you have never been an agent for any of my speaking engagements. Mostly, you were absolutely right not to have been. Whenever I have been persuaded to be master of ceremonies at some presentation or glamorous business evening, which I have done solely because the money was so nice, I have realised within a few seconds of getting on my feet that I am not a driver of men, a cheerleader or a flag-waver. I am also a mediocre after-dinner speaker. What I am very good at is not the twenty-minute quick-fire gag routine, but the leisurely talk lasting an hour or more, of the placid kind you deliver at literary festivals. Twenty minutes with Miles Kington I find very hard. Two hours with Miles Kington is no problem.

This is completely opposite to my writing experience, where I am always better over the sprint distance and no good at the long distance. I could never write a novel. If I have ever attempted a long book, it was always by dint of composing shorter pieces and joining them together seamlessly. Or, more likely, seamfully.

Anyway, I was thinking about my farewell video the other day and wondering what, if I were a member of the congregation, I would most want and expect from a posthumous video. There you are, feeling sorrowful, wishing you had seen more of your old mate before he popped his clogs, trying to concentrate on the fact that you will never ever see him again, when suddenly – the monitor in the pulpit or the screen on the wall or the huge TV screen fizzes into action and there IS your old friend again! You are seeing him again! Your dear old chum, on screen, smiles, and says: 'Sorry I couldn't be with you in person today ...'

And everyone laughs in a spooky sort of way.

It's pretty miraculous.

He's dead.

But there he is, up on the wall, smiling and saying polished things, and (if he still has any sense of timing) leaving a space for the laughs.

It's almost as if your friend is speaking to you from beyond the grave.

Given which, it would be quite nice if your late friend did give you some news from beyond the grave, you feel.

Just a hint of what life is like up there.

After all, it seems a shame for me to go to all the lengths of preparing a message from the other side, and then not saying anything about the other side at all.

So if and when I get round to writing my farewell message, I think I should drop a few hints.

One idea which occurred to me was to cut from me talking, to the door of a restaurant.

The door opens and a white-clad waiter appears.

Waiter: 'Do you have a reservation, sir?'
Me: Mumble, mumble.
Waiter: 'What name, please, sir?'
Me: Mumble, mumble.
Waiter (looking at list): 'The late Mr Miles Kington? Ah, yes, we are expecting you. Come in, please, sir.'
Me (turning to camera): 'Yes, I'm glad to report they look after you very well up here ...'

What do you think?

Love,
Miles

The Funeral Video – 3

Dear Gill,

In my last letter about my funeral video I said that people sitting in memorial congregations or audiences must be wishing most of the time that they had seen more of or talked more to the late lamented. I remember thinking this about Humphrey Carpenter. I remember thinking this about Richard Boston. I remember thinking this about Barry Took. And yet it has no effect on my present behaviour. I feel the same about Terry Jones, and Barry Cryer, and Richard Ingrams, and Posy Simmonds, and Deborah Moggach, and many other lovely people who I should have seen a lot more of *and who are all still alive*, and what am I doing about it to know them better? Not a lot.

It cuts the other way too.

I had a great mate once called Nigel Stanger, who was the best musician on the jazz scene at Oxford when I was there, playing saxophone and piano equally well. He got together a piano trio in 1962 to play in a nightclub in Spain, during our long summer vacation, in a small village in the Bay of Algeciras, with him on piano, me on double bass and a guy called Mike Hollis on drums. It was the best holiday I have ever had in my life. Nigel went off to work in the music scene in the 1960s, passing through the bands of people like Alan Price, but had a bad time with drugs and was hauled back by his parents to his native Newcastle to get clean, give up the musical life and train as an architect. Of course nobody really gives up the musical life, and he kept playing in Geordie bands, including the one in which Sting got his first break. ('I taught Sting to read music,' he told me once.)

I saw him occasionally over the years, not nearly often enough.

Then suddenly one day in the late 1980s he rang me at home from Newcastle for no ostensible reason and talked to me for three quarters of an hour. All about his plans for life in Newcastle, his partnership with local hero Chas Chandler, his passionate dislike of the Newcastle United power bosses, his children, music, his ex-wife Germaine, and the old days, and I didn't understand (being thick) why he was saying all this until I heard a month or two later that he had died, and I realised suddenly that he had rung up to say goodbye to me, knowing that he hadn't got long (it was leukaemia, I think) but that he couldn't bring himself to tell me about his approaching death or even that he was ill at all.

It reminds me of a man I once invented in my column.

I have a long-running feature called 'People With Very Unusual Jobs Indeed', and whenever I think of someone with an implausibly implausible job, I do an 'interview' with them. Like, I once invented a chap at an airport who stood with the other people in the security zone, whose sole function was to determine the gender of passengers. This was in case they had to be searched. When a passenger has to be searched, it has to be done by someone of the same sex. But what if you can't tell what sex they are? And guess wrongly? What happens if, by mistake, you get a woman to search a rather effete young man? Or a man to body-search an extremely butch lesbian? You infringe their human rights and get put in prison in Brussels, that's what. So you need a 'passenger-sexer'.

That's by the by. On another occasion I invented a man whose sole business was running an agency which interviewed people's elderly relatives before they died.

This was based on the quantity of people who had said to me over the years: 'Oh, if only I had talked properly to my father before he died! I always meant to explore his war experiences with him, and I now bitterly regret never taking the plunge ...' and similarly with their mothers, though not with so much emphasis on the war. And they never had. Because they had ignored the basic rule of interviewing, which is that it is always done best by a stranger, not by someone well known to the victim, and we always open up more to someone we think we will never see again.

Hence this fictional man with his agency, which interviewed interesting old relatives, and got it down on paper and film and audiotape.

The extraordinary thing is that after I had written this fanciful piece, I got several letters from people in the desperate situation of not knowing quite how to go about talking to their aged parents, asking as a matter of urgency to be put in touch with this agency, so they could use their services.

I am not sure what the conclusion is.

Whether someone should start such an agency?

Or whether one could write a book explaining how these things are best done, whether it's you talking to Nigel, or Nigel talking to you.

Dying for a Chat, perhaps.

And perhaps not.

Love,
Miles

The Man Who Had a Flower in His Teeth

Dear Gill,

One of the most exciting times of my life was my gap year in 1960. I didn't really plan for a gap year – I don't think gap years even existed back then – but I had to stay an extra winter term at school to take a scholarship exam (I think) and found myself at Christmas 1959 with nothing definite to do before my arrival at Oxford the following September.

Nine months with nothing to do!

After the first month, my father was getting impatient with my presence round the house.

'Are you going to *do* something?'

'How do you mean, *do* something?'

'Well, it would be a good chance to go somewhere. Why not go travelling?'

'Yes, Dad.'

Pause.

'Like, where to, Dad?'

'Oh, for heaven's sake!'

But he came up with a great idea for me. He knew someone who knew about Geest Bananas, and knew that you could hire a cabin on one of their banana boats going out to the West Indies.

'Once you get to the West Indies, you could go and stay with our friends the Strongs in Dominica. Then with Aunty Peggy in the Bahamas …'

Aunty Peggy was married to Uncle Dennis, who ran a hotel in Nassau.

'… After that, you could make your way to America and get a job and make some money, and come back home in time for university …'

Which is exactly how it all happened. I took ship with the banana boat in Barry Docks in South Wales. The crew was entirely German. I was the only passenger on board. Day after day I sat and looked at the sea and was never bored once, especially when we got into flying fish territory. Luckily I had just finished doing German A levels, so I could talk to the officers and crew – not that I ever saw anything of them, except for the gay blond steward who theoretically spent all his time looking after me, but in fact despised me because I was younger than him, and because he was German and I was British. (He actually said to me once: 'You won the war, you know, but we will win the peace.')

The officers allowed me to join them for breakfast. German-style maritime breakfast was not a comfort zone. It incorporated black bread, raw dried onions, chopped tomatoes and salami. That was about it.

'So how are we feeling this morning, Herr Kington?' one of them would say. 'Not showing any signs of sea-sickness yet?'

'No, I'm fine,' I would say stoutly, however I really felt.

'Have some more onions,' they would suggest.

There was quite a good little library on board, all in German, which is how I came to read *Black Mischief* by Evelyn Waugh for the first time in German, not English. I must have been quite good in German by the time we got to the other side – one of the officers told me that I had got a strong Westphalian accent, but I never established whether this was a good thing to have or not – and then I didn't need a word of German till I got to Oxford, not even in New York, where I ended up working for four months or so.

This was about the time, just to locate it in history, when they were gearing up for the presidential election, when Kennedy faced Nixon. Do you remember what the big question of the time was? Not, will a black man ever run for president? Or, will we ever have a female president in the USA? But, will the American public ever elect a Catholic as president? There was a lingering feeling that having a Catholic was going a step too far, that Washington would be ruled from the Vatican … Well, as we all know, they had a Catholic president without too much worry, but we still don't know about the black or the woman. Or, indeed, whether the Americans are ready for an agnostic, or worse …

I also remember going to the New York premiere of *Psycho*, and being shocked like everyone else by the shower scene – though I don't think I actually screamed quite like everyone else …

I've just remembered.

Somewhere in a bar in Greenwich Village in 1960, I saw a graffiti in the gents' loo:

MAO FOR PRESIDENT!

Someone else had written underneath:

GOOD MAN, BUT THINK OF THE RELIGIOUS PROBLEM.

The whole experience, from Barry to New York, would be worth writing about, which I have never done, but I have one special reason for remembering it now, when I have been thinking more about incurable diseases than heretofore.

Most of my evenings in New York I spent on my own, which I was happy to do, especially as I was in the HQ of jazz, where all the great men came through playing sooner or later, so I explored the jazz clubs of New York as much as one impecunious English gap-year student can.

I saw films too, and got to the theatre a bit. (I

remember going to see one of the off-Broadway hits of the season, *The Connection*, by Jack Gelber, all about jazz and drugs, a daring play then, and good stuff too.) And I discovered The Actors Studio, which was the drama place run by Lee Strasberg, where the Method actors came from; this was of no particular interest to me except that they mounted in-house productions from time to time, which I was tempted to go and see.

It might have been there, though I don't think it was, that I went to see Jack MacGowran in Beckett's *Krapp's Last Tape*, which was electrifying, though it still didn't settle the question for me of whether I liked Beckett, a question which I am still undecided over.

And one night I went to see a play by Luigi Pirandello called *The Man Who Had a Flower in His Teeth*. I knew nothing about the play. I didn't know much about Pirandello. I still don't. *Six Characters in Search of an Author* is still the only play for which he is well remembered, except in my case, where I remember *The Man Who Had a Flower in His Teeth* rather better.

It was a monologue for one man, and didn't last very long. Half an hour? Something like that. The man just talked about his life. How he enjoyed watching people, noticing things. One of the things you would notice about him, he suggested, is that he had a strange pattern in his teeth, a growth a bit like a flower. It was a tumour of some kind. It was not

107

removable, nor operable, nor curable. It was in fact fatal. He had only a few months left to live. That was why he loved watching people. All the things he had been in too much of a hurry to notice, all his life, he now slowed down to observe.

For instance, he said, I was passing by a shop the other day and slowed down to watch someone wrap a purchase for a customer. It was quite a superior shop, selling hand-made chocolates or something similar, so the person was taking a great deal of care over the wrapping, which had to be good enough for a gift.

It was a wonderful pleasure, he said, watching the care and *love* with which the person handled that plain brown paper, the way they smoothed it and flattened it and folded it. The noise it made, the faint but rich crunching sound as he tucked it and tied it and knotted it. It was a performance, and he was the only spectator at this wonderful ritual …

When you know you are going to die, you value everything much more highly, that was the message. Don't take anything for granted any more. Don't assume that things happen of their own accord. Look at things. Touch them. Smell them. (Did he describe the smell of wrapping paper? I can't remember.) And don't wait till you're dying to do it!

That was the message, I guess, of this really quite simple one-man piece, which, by the way, I have never come across in any shape or form since then.

I am not sure that it has much of a message for me right now. I think that if that Pirandello play ever had an effect on me, it was during the rest of my life, when I have found myself from time to time engrossed by simple procedures, or enjoying touching things. Old furniture. Feet on statues. The outlines of objects. The curves on radio sets – conkers, while they are still shiny and young. The shapes in ice cream …

Never mind about all that. Looking back, it isn't Pirandello that is important. It's my few months in New York. Because it was such a great and novel experience for me, I still remember lots of it very sharply, and would like while I still have the chance to write it all down. It's like coming across a box of photos called 'New York, 1960', and knowing that it is all undiscovered stuff. I didn't go to NY again for fifteen or twenty years, so my three or four month memories of the place in 1960 *can't* have been mixed up with or contaminated by memories of any similar visit …

A piece for the *New Yorker* perhaps?

I'll say one thing for Pirandello, though.

All my life I have enjoyed the smell of paper. Books and newspapers, quite; wrapping paper, a lot. Secondhand books, though, above all. You should always put your nose deep into an old book. They smell rich and strange. And they are all so different!

Not all.

Some books hardly smell at all.
But the ones that do, they repay a deep breath.
No extra charge.

Love,
Miles

Two Kinds of Books

Dear Gill,

If I am going to write a book about cancer, one thing I am going to have to bear in mind is that books about life fall generally into two camps.

There are the books that make the reader feel that the writer is far better off and far happier than the reader is or will ever be.

And there are books that make you feel that the writer has had a desperately more miserable life than you.

And both kinds of book have the effect, oddly, of cheering you up.

The first kind of book embraces all self-help books, all cookery books, all diet books, all exercise and jogging books, all therapy books – all books by people who seem to know much more about life than you do. Yet it's not really depressing to be out-cooked by Delia Smith or out-yoga'd by some guru. On the contrary. Even mastering a couple of recipes or doing some exercises will make you feel fulfilled because you have crept a little closer to the ideals of St Delia, or the physical perfection of Jane Fonda. (Did I say Jane Fonda? My God, that dates me. Who is today's Jane Fonda? Come on, agent!)

The second kind of book embraces not only all the misery memoirs, all the stories of dysfunctionalism which are so popular today, but also all the adventure, exploration, endurance and achievement books by people who have gone up Everest without oxygen or spent a long period of time cooped up with Terry Waite. People's sufferings may or may not ennoble the sufferer, but they don't half cheer up the person who didn't suffer. 'Thank God I didn't have to go through that,' you think. 'Thank God Frank McCourt or Joe Simpson did it for me.'

Joe Simpson I think is the name of the bloke who wrote *Touching the Void* or *Feeling the Void*, the book (and film) about the experience of cutting loose a rope on the other end of which dangled his friend, so that he could save his own life, and then crawling back to base with a broken leg and finding his friend there.

(A bit after that book came out there was another book by a man who was trapped in the Grand Canyon and could only escape by cutting off his own arm ...)

Enough pain.

I hate pain.

I hate reading about it.

I hate feeling it.

I think I probably hate writing about it.

As you might have guessed, I haven't read any of the misery books in the second category, so I guess I am not the ideal candidate for writing a joy-through-suffering book, a harrowing book about facing up to the reality of cancer, and coming to terms with blah blah blah blah …

I would much rather infiltrate the first group of writers, those who cheer up the reader by showing them a promised land beyond, a sunnier country than the one they live in, where every meal is perfect, every pub is an idyll and every experience is enriching and fulfilling.

Alastair Sawdayland.

National Trust Dreamland.

The Good Life Guide.

The River Café Book of Splendour.

Sounds revolting, doesn't it? And a bit depressing, too.

There is nothing more calculated to put you in a bad mood than the sight of someone you cannot measure up to. But I think that is what I have got to aim for.

Not an uplifting book about cancer.

Not even a cheery book about cancer.

But a funny book about cancer!

Think about it.

Love,
Miles

The Language of Cancer

Dear Gill,

I take your point that it is not up to you to think about it, but really much more down to me, as I may have come up with the notion of a funny book about getting cancer, but not thought of any ideas yet. Still, at least you approve in principle.

Thanks for your suggestion that today's Jane Fonda is Cindy Crawford.

Who is Cindy Crawford?

One idea for a funny book about cancer would be a look at the language of cancer.

You don't have to have spent much time inside the wonderful world of cancer to realise that they talk a different language there. For a start, they don't like to use the word 'cancer' much – and that applies to the specialists as well. There is no such thing as a 'cancer specialist' either, only an 'oncologist', which I guess is the Greek word for cancer specialist, but sounds a lot nicer.

It's almost as if they don't like to admit they're talking about cancer at all. It's not the same with venereal diseases or sexually transmitted diseases, where words like syphilis and gonorrhoea are bandied about the whole time. Come to think of it, in the world of STD they even have nicknames for these unpleasant diseases, like 'pox' and 'the clap', but there are no such short cuts in cancer. No jolly nicknames. It's all fairly grim and unsmiling there. At least, when the patient is around. When doctors are by themselves, it's bound to be different.

Right from the start, I noticed that when I was there and they were trying to tell me what I had got, they didn't use the word cancer. Words like 'carcinogenic' and 'tumour' floated around, but not the word 'cancer'. I think it was me eventually who said to one of the specialists, 'So, what it boils down to is that I have got cancer of the pancreas, have I?'

He looked quite relieved that I had brought the subject up.

(Maybe it is one of those games they play to while away the tedium of cancer care, the getting-the-patient-to-say-it-first game. I believe that barristers sometimes play a similar game in court. Opposing counsel agree beforehand that the first of them to manage to introduce into a speech an agreed word such as 'sequoia' or 'persiflage' or 'pinguid' wins the game. The police have the same kind of games too, believe it or not. In the case of the cancer people, maybe the specialist who can get the patient to say the word 'cancer' before he does gets the jackpot.)

Of course, this is a bit unfair on doctors, because everyone I know is the same. My friends – they hate to say the word 'cancer'. I didn't know John Wayne, but he was the same, too. When he was diagnosed with lung cancer, he called it 'The Big C' and said he was going to lick it. At least he thought of a name for it, even if he didn't lick it. Most of the people I know mysteriously drift into euphemism if they talk about my condition at all, and refer vaguely to 'your trouble', 'your illness', or, mostly, 'your condition'.

I guess that's because we haven't been trained to talk about illness.

All we know is that cancer is a killer, and can sometimes be cured, but mostly isn't, and is a painful way to go.

So I feel a bit of a fraud that I am not suffering much.

I get quite a lot of backache, but it isn't bad backache, just a low-level ache, and I sometimes get stomach upsets, but not badly so, and I have got pills that deal with both of them, so it would be ridiculous to ask for any sympathy at all, really. I don't want people to get the impression that I am in no discomfort at all, because they might feel a bit cheated. All I ask is that they are not shy of using the word 'cancer', so that we can refer to it if we have to, and then get on to a more interesting topic, but I am coming to realise that people think it is bad luck to mention it by name, or that it causes you pain, or makes it worse, so what they generally do is glide round the subject and take refuge in generalities ...

'How are things going, Miles?'

'How are you feeling today?'

'How's everything?'

'So, how are things going?'

'What sort of a day are you having?'

What they really mean is:

'I don't know anything about cancer.'

'I don't know how ill you are.'

'My Uncle Harry died of lung cancer, but everyone said he smoked like a chimney and had only himself to blame, and I wish I had paid more attention then because I don't really know anything about cancer ...'

'You're not going to keel over and die while I'm talking to you, are you?'

What we need is a small booklet which tells people how to talk to each other about cancer.

The Language of Cancer.

Parlez-Vous Cancer?

Incurable But Not Unsayable.

I Was Sorry To Hear About Your ... Your ... Your ...

Which I am prepared to write.

Meanwhile, I am working on a provisional plan

to deal in real life with my own inquirers about my condition, which is going to be based on the experience of encountering the pedlars who come to my house from time to time.

Being a writer, I work at home, so I am there in my house in our village most days, a prey to all casual callers. For a long time it was just Jehovah's Witnesses. (Good people, but expansive.) They have given up recently, and been replaced by gentlemen in vans selling fresh frozen fish from freeze-blasted premises. (Good, but expensive.) Recently, in the last year or two, they have tailed off as well and been replaced by young door-to-door pedlars with big bags over their shoulders.

They all have the same routine. They come down the yard, and they knock on the door and, when I appear, hold up a card to me and recite the same little litany.

'Could you spare a moment to read this, please, sir?'

And they give me the card, and I read it, and it always says, more or less: 'My name is Donald Simpson. I live in Nottingham, where I have been unable to find work. In order to try to provide for myself, I have taken to selling domestic produce from door to door. Please spend a few minutes looking at the wide range of items I have for sale.'

I know very well what those items are, even

before I look in his capacious bag. They are ironing board covers, mock-chamois leathers, oven gloves, gardening gloves, all-purpose scissors, car torches which plug in the cigarette lighter, peg bags, tea cloths, sticky tape ...

How do I know all this?

Because I have felt sorry for so many young men from Nottingham, though occasionally from Sheffield, that down in our cellar there is a large stock of all the oven gloves, aprons, tea cloths, peg bags, etc. that I have bought over the years and which we do not get through nearly so fast as I buy them. My wife now dreads the arrival of these young men in case a) I am going to buy some more stuff, or b) she will have to face them herself. The last time one of them called, which was in late October, my wife saw him coming down the yard first and a) pushed me to the door to answer it, and b) hissed in my ear: 'Don't buy *anything*!' He was from Middlesbrough, which was nice for a change, but I didn't buy anything. He said: 'Please buy something! It's my first week!' I felt myself wobble, but I heard myself say, 'Oh, they all say that!' What a bastard.

So now I have decided to bypass these painful conversations by having a special card printed. After I have read his card, I will produce mine and say, 'I have read your card. Now you take a minute to read this.'

My card will read as follows: 'Thank you for

letting me read your card. Sympathetic as I am to your situation, I must tell you that I have had many previous young visitors from the North over the years, and have purchased many items from them, most of them still unused. Before I see the contents of your bag, I invite you to survey the wide range of purchases in my cellar, including oven gloves, garden kneeling pads, secateurs, etc., etc. If anything catches your eye, you are welcome to make an offer.'

That should do it.

Similarly, when people ask me after my condition, I am now determined to hand them a card which says:

'Thank you for asking after my condition. I have been diagnosed with cancer of the pancreas, which is, as a doctor friend of mine said comfortingly, not one of the nice ones. It cannot be operated on, apparently, and although they can give you chemotherapy, which I have already started, it will only slow the process down, and I will be very lucky if it arrests it. On the bright side, it doesn't seem to be one of the very painful forms of cancer, unless they've been holding out on me. One specialist said I might last for years, and I would only know it was finally coming to get me when I started gently fading away, like a torch in a tent at night with a battery which was coming near to the end of its life. Rather a nice image for a gastro-enterologist, I thought. Anyway, that's how things are. Up and down. Over and out.'

I just hope I don't get the cards mixed up, and hand the door-to-door brush-off to a close friend, or the cancer card to a young stranger from Nottingham.

Anyway, that's the idea for the book ...

I Was Sorry To Hear About Your ... Your ... Your ...

Over to you.

Love,
Miles

Policemen's Games

Dear Gill,

You ask me what these games are that policemen play.

Well, I live in a small village near Bath, as you know, and one day, about four years after we first moved in, I saw my very first police presence in the village.

It was a police car moving slowly down the main street, which slowed even further when it saw me, and followed me at walking pace.

I stopped.

It stopped.

'Do you live here?' said the driver.

'Yes,' I said, feeling unaccountably threatened.

The driver looked at me earnestly.

'Where are we?' he said.

He was lost.

Years later I met a policeman off duty at a party and told him this story.

'He might not have been just lost,' he said. 'He might have been playing the Met Game.'

'The Met Game?'

'You know that the Met is the Metropolitan Force – the London police?'

'Y-e-e-s …'

'Well, when they get really bored with daily routine, they have one or two games or competitions they can resort to, and that's one of them, seeing how far you can drive out of London and back in the same day. I was once stopped in Bath by a pair of policemen from London and asked to sign a certificate saying they'd been to Bath. I believe Paris and back in the day is the record, actually.'

This cast the police in a new and more sympathetic light for me. Especially when I was telling this story to someone else at another party, and they said, 'Oh, a bit like the Motorway Police Game.'

?????

'You don't know it? Oh, apparently when the motorway traffic police get really bored with the repetitive tedium of arresting people for speeding, they sometimes introduce snooker rules.'

Snooker rules?

'Yes. They arrest a red car, then another colour, then another red car, then another colour, and so on through the colours till they get to black. First to clear the table wins.'

There's another book there, I think. On the great secret games of all the professions. Or a TV programme. Or radio at least.

At the very least, a short article entitled 'Why People Who Drive Red Cars Should Drive Ten Times More Carefully Than Anyone Else.'

Love,
Miles

Royalties

Dear Gill,

It may not be too late to make my fortune. I should have told you about it a bit earlier, that's all.

When I went to see *Jeffrey Bernard Is Unwell*, the smash-hit play by Ned Sherrin with Peter O'Toole, I was amazed when, to emphasise Bernard's hopeless way with deadlines, a plump little actor carried on a bit of paper and read out, 'Dear Jeffrey, Are you going to write the fucking article or aren't you? Yours, Miles Kington, *Punch*!' He then walked off again.

This was a genuine letter I had written to Jeffrey, and at the time I just felt flattered to hear it included in the play. But it slowly dawned on me over the years that if it was quoted every night wherever and whenever it was performed, there might be something due to me for it.

For six or seven seconds my words were being quoted in a West End play.

I had written a line of dialogue in a smash hit.

Even if it only got me 5p a time, that would easily add up to a sizeable royalty.

Now that Ned Sherrin has gone, I am not sure the position is any different. If I was owed a bit of money, presumably there is a kitty out of which I can get paid.

How do you feel, O agent?

Love,
Miles

Board Games

Dear Gill,

How about death and board games?

There hasn't been a good new board game since … since …

Is Trivial Pursuit a board game?

I'm not sure it is.

Of all the board games I have seen come and go in my life, the old favourites still remain. Chess. Draughts. Monopoly. Cluedo. Snakes and Ladders. Scrabble.

There must be life in Monopoly yet, as I still see grown-ups get deeply involved in it, and it can't all be nostalgia. And they still bring out new versions of Monopoly, with the familiar sites replaced by streets in your local town (they've even got a Bath version in my neck of the woods) or other gimmicks.

So how about a board game which confronted death?

Necropoly, for instance.

The winner would be the first player who died, lay in state for weeks, had a state funeral, and was laid to rest in a mausoleum grand enough to bankrupt the country.

Or you could have a game based on death in more familiar domestic detail, where you start with someone else's death and the whole game is all about deciding what kind of funeral the late lamented would have wanted, who gets all the money, who has to be the wretched executor, and what to do with the player who presents the card saying: 'I am the illegitimate daughter spawned in Canada in his youth, and I can prove it, so I demand my share of the estate!'

If the game was anything like real life, the players would all end up bitter enemies and not talking to each other.

It's curious, though, that lots of games are about dying, but none about the ceremony of death. In war games, whole armies are wiped out. My brother and I used to play endless encounters of an air, sea and land battle game called Tri-tactics, in which you could hardly move without sinking a ship or eliminating squads of men. It never occurred to us that we were killing people. Nowadays, in video games, the killing is all more graphic and horrible, but it is still stylised, so that even though the victim sprawls in agony and oozes blood, the player doesn't really feel that death is going on. There are never any medics.

Or ambulances. Or wounded people being carried to safety.

And certainly nothing to do with the ceremony of death, the process of coming to terms with it all. When was there ever a game based on a funeral? And a speech by a vicar who had clearly never met the late lamented? And the reading of the will? And the hatred of one side of the family for another? And the tears of the mourners being shed for the one person who has actually come out of this quite happily, being now either in heaven or much longed for oblivion?

Food for thought here?

Love,
Miles

PART III

The Descent

Tie-in Books

Dear Gill,

Do you remember a conversation we once had, as we strolled out of an evening, hand in hand, author and agent outlined against the setting sun … ?

No, of course you don't.

No writer and agent ever strolled hand in hand.

The most they ever do is get together for lunch, and the nearest their hands get to meeting is if they both reach for the bottle of wine at the same time.

'Sorry …'

'No, after you …'

I expect that is what we were doing, having lunch together, somewhere in the Notting Hill area, where I had lived for twenty years and thought I knew all the restaurants, though it turned out that all my favourite eating places had closed before your agency moved in, and you now knew all the good places. And half the people in them.

'Hello, Michael …'

'Hi, Gill …'

What the conversation was about was the current state of publishing.

'Publishers are receiving more and more unsolicited manuscripts,' you said. 'More than ever, they are being swamped by books they haven't asked for from people they don't know and don't want to know. It has got to the stage where publishers cannot even pretend to read all the stuff they are sent. So now they only read stuff passed on to them by agents whom they know and trust.'

I squeezed your hand.

No, I didn't.

I passed you the salt.

'That's you,' I said. 'The trustworthy agent.'

'That's me,' you said, amazed and relieved that an author could keep up with the argument. 'However, in the same sort of way as a traffic bottleneck is never cured, but only reappears a bit further down the road on someone else's patch, it is now the agents who are suffering. Knowing that publishers won't read their stuff, would-be writers are now sending it all to agents. And we can't read it all either.'

A dismal feeling came over me.

'Oh, my God,' I said. 'You're not going to offer me a job at the agency reading incoming stuff, are you?'

For just a moment a look of horror came over

your face, as you briefly envisaged the idea of a writer being allowed to hang around full-time in the office.

'Good God, no,' you said. 'What I was going to say was that in future we are going to ask our writers not to submit an entire new book, but an idea for a book, plus a sample of how you intend to write it. Not a long sample. Just a sample.'

'Nice idea,' I said, as I paused to admire the sunset and you asked to have a look at the dessert menu. 'But it's pretty risky.'

'Risky? How?'

'Well, you might find that some of your writers, even your best writers, are better at thinking up ideas than writing books. You could end up with a lot of commissioned books which are never going to be written because the writer could do the sales pitch better than the execution. I have been guilty of that in my time …'

'Hmmmmm …'

'And you're also in danger of landing yourself with books which sounded like a good idea at the time, but which grow into books which nobody wants or needs. It happens every day in the papers, on a smaller scale. Open any paper and you will find articles written because the editorial meeting thought it would be a good idea to have a topic covered badly rather than not at all, so they rang up some poor wage hack and said, "Do a thousand words on famous writers who have fallen in love with football by 3.30 this afternoon."

'Same with books. Every week a book comes out because it seemed a good idea at the time to have a centenary book on Auden, or a new history of cannibalism in the South Seas, or a record of the British Lions' Tour of Down Under, or Lindy Travis's own life story ...'

'Who is Lindy Travis?' you said, as I hoped you would.

'Oh, she's the latest gardening woman on TV,' I said. 'Bit of a sex bomb. She bends over the herbs and spices bed in a rather provocative manner. She has become sensationally popular on TV ever since the rumours started that she might be having a secret affair with Delia Smith.'

'Delia Smith!'

'Or do I mean Gordon Ramsay?'

'Heavens,' you said, 'she sounds dynamite! There hasn't been a sexy gardener since Charlie what's-her-name ... I'm surprised I've never heard of Lindy Travis.'

'I'm not,' I said. 'I just made her up.'

You aimed a playful blow at me and drew blood.

'I'm just trying to make the point that Lindy Travis sounds like a good idea for a book,' I said. 'Sexy TV gardener. It's usually the cooks who are dishy. And the hint of a flirtation with another TV guru, across the disciplines! From cooking to gardening! That would be a first. The only snag is that it is all fiction. And you fell for it.'

'Which leaves me incredibly depressed,' you said, ordering a crème brûlée to cheer yourself up. 'The fact that I could see a book in what is, at most, a gossip column item. What happened to the book world I came into?'

'It vanished,' I said. 'It started to vanish the first time somebody said, "Let's do the book of the ..." '

'The book of what?'

'Book of anything. It doesn't matter what. The first time someone thought a tie-in book would make money.'

'But that has been going on for years!' you said. 'It's not a new idea. Every time an exhibition pro-duces a catalogue, you've got a tie-in book. Every time someone does something heroic or unexpected, and someone else writes a book about it ... Stanley and Livingstone ... all those Captain Scott books about how Scott got there and didn't quite make it back ...'

'All those Amundsen books written in Sweden about the man who got there first and did get back, which for some reason or other have never become classics in Britain, or even been translated as far as I know ...'

'What about J. M. Barrie?' you said.

'What about him?'

'Well, the Peter Pan and Wendy story was a stage hit. A huge stage hit. It wasn't a book at all. Nobody ever really rushes out and buys the script of the play. So in order to give the public a book-of-the-show to buy, Barrie actually had to physically sit down and write it out all over again as a story. Nowadays we'd call it a "novelisation" and we'd be a bit sniffy about it. Not then, it seems. Anyway it made Barrie a fortune.'

'Interesting,' I said.

There was a silence. The sky started to go dark, and the last pink drained away. The waiter cleared away the coffee cups.

'Well,' I said, 'this has not been entirely wasted. You wanted to explain the changing face of publishing to me, which you have done, and you wanted me to come up with an idea for a book, which I have done ...'

'Have you? I didn't notice.'

'Yes,' I said. 'An idea for a history of the tie-in book.'

You turned it over in your mind.

'Run that past me again,' you said.

'Well,' I said, waxing expansive and thinking big – in other words, improvising wildly, 'if you accept the Bible as the tie-in book for Christianity, and the Koran as the same for Islam; if you see the Bayeux Tapestry as the coffee-table book of the Norman Invasion; if we skate lightly over stained glass church windows as picture books for the illiterate; if you view *Das Kapital* and *Scouting for Boys* as the souvenir publications of two very different youth movements; then you can see that there is a great deal more to the history of the tie-in book than is suggested by the names Alan Titchmarsh and Michael Palin.'

'I like it,' you said, placing your credit card on top of the bill. 'Could you put that down in writing and let me have it as a proposal?'

I said I would, and now, albeit somewhat belatedly, I have.

Love,
Miles

The Way You Look

Dear Gill,

Has anyone ever written a book called something like 'The Way You Think You Look, and The Way You *Really* Look'?

It might be subtitled something like 'How things got that way, and what you can do about it', or 'what you can *still* do about it'.

I don't think so. And yet it centres on one of the puzzles that haunt all of us, which is that we have all gone through phases of looking quite good, and that even if we think we still do, then catching sight of ourselves in the mirror, now and then, unawares, will reveal the awful truth to us: that person staring back at us out of the mirror is not the person we imagine ourselves to be when we are mirror-free, the rest of the time.

I myself, for instance, used to be quite good-looking, perhaps for twenty years and upwards. I didn't realise it at the time, but I think I was, if only because quite a lot of women I knew then say to me now, 'You were very dishy in those days, you know,' and I only wish I had known they thought that then.

Anyway, for a long part of my life I thought I looked nothing special, though apparently I did, and as I grew in confidence in my forties I began to think, well, perhaps I *do* present a handsome mien to the world. (Mien – a word I have never used out loud, as along with gewgaw and some others, I am not sure how it is pronounced.) And as I began to have more confidence in my appearance, so my appearance began to fade, so that for most of my life I have had an idea of the way I look which was utterly wrong, first because I thought I looked dowdy and didn't, and latterly because I thought I looked OK but had become dowdy with age.

I suspect that women have a shrewder idea of how they really look, and that although they would still flock to buy a book called *The Way You Think You Look, And the Way You REALLY Look*, they would know most of it already. That is why women, on the whole, dress either to compensate for their weak points or to emphasise their strong points, or, with luck, both.

Women who are too chubby, for instance, and who have given up all idea of dieting themselves back into shape, learn how to adopt clothes which disguise their portliness and often give them a floating stateliness which is quite becoming. Thin women who are never going to put on weight learn how to capitalise on their thinness and turn it into slimness.

Even better, women are quite adept at working out which is their best feature and how to enhance it. Just as they may be made miserable by the thought of their worst feature (My big nose! My mole! My tiny bosom! My clod-hopping feet!), so they can be cheered up for all time by the thought of their best feature.

I used to know Tina Brown slightly when she was starting out on her rise to fame, and was always struck by the way she disguised her face, if not concealed it. She had a big fringe. She wore big sunglasses. If she had been able to get away with a false moustache, she would have. As it was, the eyes were led downwards to her décolletage, where her two breasts were always on striking display, like lustrous huge antique light bulbs in a Portobello Road shop. I don't know if she preferred people (men) to look at her bosom rather than her face, but the result was that although she had quite a striking face, you could never remember what she looked like, only what her bosom looked like.

Another woman I remember meeting from those times was the then Arianna Stassinopoulos, who later married an American with a silly but pronounceable name, but at that time was accompanying Bernard Levin here and there. I met her at the *Punch* lunch. Not sure I didn't sit next to her. She seemed to have decided that her eyes were her best feature, as she had affixed to them false eyelashes of quite profound weight and stature which she fluttered constantly, like a pair of captive butterflies. I won't swear to it, but in retrospect it seemed as if she worked her eyelashes so hard, you could hear them slightly, and feel a slight draught from them.

If there is any truth in my theory, then here were two women who had divined what made them striking and had decided to play down all their other features to highlight the main one, as if they were putting the main actor of the piece in the best possible place on stage. 'Nose? Eyes? Mouth? Do not upstage bosom!' 'Facial features? Stand back and let the eyes have all the applause! One day it will be your turn, I promise. Well, not you, chin. The Stassinopoulos chin is not star-quality material, I fear ...'

What has all this got to do with cancer? Nothing, I am afraid. I just think there is a good idea for a book here. Oh, and I have started to notice that my neck doesn't take ties any more. I have always quite enjoyed wearing the occasional tie, because over the years Caroline has bought me half a dozen stunningly striped hand-painted ties made by Victoria Richards which are so eye-catching that they are a pleasure to wear, knowing that this would draw comments. (From Richard Whiteley once, whose style was his ties: 'Like the tie, Mr Kington!' at Fowey Book Festival.) But the last few times I have donned my ties, like a knight issuing in the lists in his heraldic colours, I have noticed that my neck, no doubt suffering the same weight loss as the rest of my body, has gone scraggy and doesn't take ties well.

Would *The Way You Think You Look, and The Way You REALLY Look* help to solve this problem?

As I don't think I'll be writing the book, I don't really mind either way. But to whoever does write the book, I recommend it as a small but interesting problem.

Love,
Miles

Assassination – 1

Dear Gill,

On one of the cookbook shelves in our kitchen there is a small framed photograph which just sits there, mostly unnoticed. But when it does come to be noticed by the wandering eye of a stranger, it tends to produce a gasp.

It's in black and white. It shows two people sitting facing the camera, side by side on a bench. The middle-aged man on the left is wearing shorts and a small white pointed beard. The girl on the right is a prettyish smiling teenager, with plaits. The man, who looks quite glamorous, like a mid-period portrait of Ernest Hemingway, has one hand resting on the snout of an animal standing in front of them. It is a small rhinoceros. Everyone's eyes, including possibly the rhino's, are on the camera.

The girl is my wife, Caroline, and the photo was taken when she went out to Africa in the early 1960s to stay for a while with her father, who is the glamorous man in shorts, and have a wonderful time there. She hardly knew him at all. He had been in tanks all during the war and, driven crazy by post-war austerity and boredom, had re-enlisted in the Army after she was born and ended up back in Africa, though now in Kenya. After his soldier days were over, he stayed out there and worked in wild animal preservation and, to be honest, seemed to have devoted more of his active life to safeguarding rhino, hippos and elephants than to his wife and family.

Caroline did not see a lot of him again after that blissful trip to Kenya. Nick – his name was Nick Carter – drifted further and further down the African continent, through Mozambique to South Africa, where his final post was as the warden of a dwindling herd of elephants in Knysna Forest, which was, I believe, the last native herd of elephants in the country. Nick got married again to a South African woman called Gillian, and when I met Caroline in about 1980 I don't think she had seen Nick since that trip to Kenya nearly twenty years earlier.

She had never lost touch, though, and we went out to South Africa on several occasions to stay with them in Knysna, so that Nick could get a look at her second husband, and vice versa. I think Nick and I got on very well. We had similar senses of humour. We both enjoyed boisterous pointless arguments, endlessly manoeuvring the other round to boggy territory.

We liked talking about sport. He had published several books in his time, so he loved talking to me about writing and I loved pretending I knew lots about it. Although he had had a fairly horrendous time in the North African desert in the Tank Regiment, where he had seen some of his best friends killed, he was still fascinated by war, and especially by the Falklands campaign, which was just under way when I first met Caroline, and most of his best stories were about either war or wildlife.

'I remember once,' he told me, 'waking up in North Africa in a tank drawn up with lots of other British tanks on one side of a big sandy valley, facing a line of German tanks way over on the other side of the valley. But before any engagement could take place, the RAF flew over with a squadron of bombers and let rip. Unfortunately, they got the sides wrong, and dropped all their bombs on us. I swear you could just hear the Germans cheering in the distance. Didn't last for long, though. The Luftwaffe came over next, saw what the RAF had done to us, assumed we were the Germans, and proceeded to bombard their own side. That's war for you.'

By the time I met him, he was getting quite old, though he was still impressively white-haired and handsome. He insisted that washing your hair was bad for it, as it removed all the natural oils, and he claimed that he had not shampooed his own for forty years. Instead, he gave it a drastic combing and brushing every day. It certainly shone. And although he was getting on in years, he had not entirely given up all thought of active service.

'If I have one ambition left,' he told us once, 'it is to go out and do an assassination.'

'Anyone particular?' we asked him idly.

'I think it would have to be Colonel Gaddafy,' he said.

This shook us slightly, as he had never expressed any dislike of Gaddafy before, and although he did have extreme prejudices against certain people, they usually turned out to be Afrikaners, usually locals or tourists or just people running the country. He didn't like Afrikaners much. So why Gaddafy? What made him the perfect victim?

'It isn't so much that Gaddafy is the perfect victim,' said Nick, 'as that I am the perfect assassin.'

Expounding his theory, he explained that in his experience assassins were all youngish fanatical men (or youngish ruthless men who needed money very badly) and none of them were ever elderly people with a twinkle in their eye. Like himself.

'Nobody would ever suspect me,' he said. 'Here I am, near the end of my life, getting feebler, but thanks to the army and wildlife fully capable of handling a gun and using it. I haven't got long for the world. There is still one useful job in me. Why not make it a really special one and get myself hired to knock off someone that no one likes?'

The odd thing was that Nick himself did not dislike Gaddafy particularly, if at all. Politically I think he was quite agnostic about foreign statesmen, though domestically he was pretty conservative. Did he like Mrs Thatcher? He must have done. I don't see how he could not have done. And he certainly did not dislike Gaddafy on religious grounds, as Nick had done a lot of questioning of religion through his life and sometimes been quite heavily attracted to other beliefs. Buddhism, I think, had taken his fancy as a religion for a long while, though I could not resist starting one of our arguments by maintaining that Buddhism, by doing without a god, was not one of your proper religions.

'Ah, that is what a lot of people say who haven't looked closely at Buddhism,' he said, 'but let me tell you that ...'

And we would be off again.

Islam he found a bit of a poser, and although he saw it as a very respectable heavyweight religion, he also liked to back the underdog and heavily sided with Salman Rushdie when it came to a showdown between Rushdie and Islam. I remember suggesting to him that if he turned his attention away from Colonel Gaddafy and thought about exterminating Salman Rushdie instead, and actually knocked off the contentious author, he would be in the unexpected position of becoming a champion of the Muslim world over-night, even if it might also endanger his old British Army pension rights. Even Mrs Thatcher might jib at paying a pension to Nick the Jackal.

'No,' he said. 'Couldn't kill Salman Rushdie. He's guarded night and day by two highly trained British agents. Out of my league, old boy.'

The fact that Colonel Gaddafy was simultaneously guarded by the entire Libyan secret service and intelligence forces didn't seem quite so daunting to him somehow, and to the end of his days he never gave up the idea that he could have been the chosen one to get rid of the father of the Libyan nation. (I wonder if, having fought in North Africa during the war, he thought he still knew his way round Libya better than most?) I have never asked his wife, now his widow, Gillian, what she thought about all this, as she is a very sincere church-going Christian and must have had real misgivings about his plan to murder Gaddafy. Or perhaps she did not take it quite as seriously as he did.

Well, she is still alive, and so is Gaddafy, even if Nick isn't, and perhaps I am the only person who fondly remembers his theory that of all people in the world the ideal assassin is an elderly gent with not long to live, few scruples and short of a bob or two. Nice idea, though, don't you think?

Love,
Miles

Assassination – 2

Dear Gill,

As you shrewdly point out, I ended my last letter with the thought 'A nice idea, eh?', or words to that effect, without actually bothering to spell out the idea I was trying to get across.

Well, whatever the final idea would be, it would come directly from this idea of my father-in-law Nick Carter that the ideal person to carry out a high-level assassination would be an elderly person with not long to live and nothing to lose.

Nick lived in hopes that someone would come along one day and hire him to bump Gaddafy off. Not very strong hopes. He never advertised his services. He talked about it freely, but never to the sort of people who might be interested in getting rid of Gaddafy, only to his equally idle fellow café habitués in Knysna, South Africa, where he lived. Caroline and I, his daughter and son-in-law, never tried to dissuade him from bumping off Gaddafy, because we thought it was more important to try to persuade him to write down his memoirs, from his nightmare yet exciting life in tanks in wartime North Africa to his pioneering days in wildlife conservation in East Africa in the 1950s.

And they were pioneering, too. One of the biggest jobs for anyone looking after rhinos is giving them medical attention, which cannot be done until they are unconscious and out for the count. So Nick set to devising a method of rendering rhinos unconscious which involved firing a hypodermic syringe at them from a crossbow. Held by him. In a helicopter. Yes, he would actually circle round the rhinoceros in a helicopter waiting for a good moment to shoot it full of anaesthetic from a crossbow. There are not many good moments for this. But it worked often enough for it to be accounted successful (perhaps all other methods were just so much worse), and he gained notoriety as 'Carter the Darter'. There was even an early nature TV programme made about him, which still resides in the vaults of an East Anglian TV company and turns up on the TV every ten years. It's Nick Carter himself all right, except for the voice, which to everyone's surprise is a dubbed-on Australian actor.

Other rare parts of his life turned up in his rich repertoire of anecdotes, such as his brief life with J. B. Priestley. He liked to tell us how after the war, before re-enlisting in the Army, he thought he might make a go of it as a farmer, and so got a job, to learn the ropes, on the workforce of Mr Priestley's farm on the Isle of Wight. It didn't take being there for long to convince him that he disliked the farming life, disliked J. B. Priestley even more, and disliked Jacquetta Hawkes most of all. The only part of the life he enjoyed was mixing with the horny-handed sons of toil who worked on the farm, though they must have found him a strange intruder from the big world, coming straight from tanks to tractors as he did.

We never had any luck in getting him to write all this down. It wasn't the case, as it is with most people, that he could not write or did not know how to, which seldom stops people anyway. The fact was that he *could* write and had several books to his name to prove it. A novel or two, and a book of East African adventures called *The Arm'd Rhinoceros*. So why didn't he take the next not very drastic step and plunge into the composition of a late life memoir?

Well, I think possibly because he had already turned it into a successful monologue. All the best stories, the best bits, had been transformed into single performance pieces which he delivered wonderfully in company, and the more polished the best anecdotes became, the harder it would have been to string them together as a logical sequence, and the gaps between the jewels might have been as obtrusive as the jewels themselves. Might he not have thought to himself that if he ever wrote it all down, all his friends would say to themselves, 'Well, we've heard all the best bits before and the other bits aren't as good as the best bits …'

(Great error, incidentally. To think a book has to have only best bits. A book which had only best bits would be unbearable.)

I still wonder, though, if there might not be some good juice left in his idea of an elderly or infirm person volunteering an assassination as his last useful act on earth.

Me. For instance.

Look at me.

Cancer.

Doomed.

Beyond suspicion.

People who look at my hangdog expression and my air of lingering malady would never dream that underneath it all simmers a potential killer.

A man for hire.

I am surely the last man in the world whom you would suspect of being a killer, as nobody ever heard of a humorous writer being man enough to go out and kill people.

I know that people sometimes shake their heads sagely and say we all have it within us to commit brutal acts of torture and murder. When we condemn

Argentinian secret police or Nazi torturers for crimes against humanity, there will always be someone else on the other side of the public bar to say, 'Ah, but how do we know how *we* would react if called upon to eliminate a fellow human being?'

I know how I would react now.

I'd think of Nick, and jump at the chance.

Give me a victim and I will rub them out.

I don't care any longer!

What can they do to me in return?

Give me a life sentence?

I already have a life sentence!

(I am dramatising this in ways which do not come naturally to me, and which I feel I would have to practise …)

Obviously this is something we would have to discuss quite confidentially, as the hallmark of assassination is secrecy, but if you like the idea of me volunteering to get rid of some public enemy and then committing the perfect murder, which will totally baffle the police, after which I would settle down to writing an account of the whole affair to leave for you to publish after my death, I think it would make a most unusual bestseller.

And I really do think it would make a bestseller.

The only snag I can see from here is that it might get you into trouble more than me.

If all went well, and my posthumous confessions

were published and everyone bought them, leaving the police feeling even more outsmarted than usual, it might occur to some unusually perceptive copper that *you* had prior knowledge of the crime and were therefore an accessory before the fact. Infuriated by not being able to get at me (I might have to insist on getting it into my contract that I should be beyond the law first, i.e. dead), they would like to search for someone to vent their wrath on and would find you and arrest you for prior knowledge. Of course, you could plead justification in that you had been partly responsible for the death of a public nuisance like Jeffrey Archer or Jordan or Victoria Beckham (or all of the Spice Girls together in one fell swoop?) or even poor old Michael Barrymore, but I fear this would not be a total defence in court.

Any thoughts so far?

Love,
Miles

Assassination – 3

Dear Gill,

You're quite right.

I deserved that.

My choice of possible murder victims was totally trivial.

I was misled by the prevailing celebrity culture into thinking that I should devote my dying days to getting rid of public irritants. What a waste of time. Even if I did settle on someone who genuinely irritated everyone, by the time I had done the deed, they would no longer be irritating. Somebody else would have the title. Imagine if I had taken it into my head to eliminate Jade Goody, who I think was the national irritant one year. When I got round to doing the deed, she would be almost forgotten, as she is now – indeed, she would be half-remembered in a sort of fond afterglow, so people would be terribly upset that she had been outed. Offed. Wasted. Whatever.

So if I am going to assassinate someone in the

public eye, it should at least be someone genuinely well-hated.

(Have you noticed that in Britain we always call a much-loved person a 'best-loved' person? 'Joanna Lumley, perhaps the best-loved person in showbiz …' Why *best*? We don't love her *well*. We love her a *lot*. She is one of the *most*-loved women in Britain. Pedant. Sorry.)

So, the kind of person I should be aiming at is a really unpopular bogeyman like … well, like Robert Maxwell used to be. If there were someone still around like him … Hold on! Rupert Murdoch! Maxwell is dead, but Rupert Murdoch is still there. And so, at the time of going to press, is Robert Mugabe.

(All with the same initials. R. M. How curious.)

Rupert Murdoch is the one I would go for first, if only because it would please my chums in the media, and make some great headlines, but I would guess that he is probably well guarded, too well guarded for an amateur like me to get at.

Perhaps this is the sort of thing an agent could handle. Literary agents tend to think that their business is restricted to sorting out contracts, and making eyes at publishers, but there comes a moment when you guys have to get down to the rock face and do some real work, so your task for today is to find out how easy it would be for an ex-employee of Murdoch (I did write a column for him for years) to get an interview with him and then pull a gun on him.

Come on, Gill!

It would make a change from long lunches.

Just asking.

Of course, I am taking it for granted that the best way to use this plot device is in real life, but maybe it is best used as a real plot device, i.e. a plot in a work of fiction. I wonder if it has ever been done, the Nick Carter idea, that is, having a murder done by someone suffering from a fatal disease and determined to right some glaring wrong before they die.

And as I write those words, I realise that that is exactly the plot line of Agatha Christie's *Ten Little Niggers*. It is years since I read that great book, when I was in my teens and went through a phase of trying to read all that great woman's thrillers, but I still remember that all the murders are done by a retired judge who has seen some real miscarriages of justice in his courts, mostly with murderers getting off scot-free, and decides to murder ten of them himself while he still can.

Using a well-known nursery rhyme as the plot link and source of ideas.

To do ten successful murders is good enough, but to get all the murder methods from a nursery rhyme deserves lots of bonus points in my book.

(Incidentally, Gill, sorry if you have never read

Ten Little Niggers, as I now seem to have given away the denouement, and thus neatly spoiled it for you, though you might be relieved that you no longer have to read it. And sorry if I don't call it *Ten Little Indians.* One of the great advantages of a limited life span is that you don't have to use an extra antenna to be politically correct all the time, any more.)

Or what about using this idea in a work based on fact? That is, re-examine a well-known murder, and come up with a brand-new theory that the culprit was actually a disgruntled old chap. Mohammed al Fayed keeps doing this, whenever he accuses the Duke of Edinburgh of being behind Diana's death. And I wonder if there were any old age pensioners on Robert Maxwell's yacht the night he slid off the end of the boat … ?

In connection with which, I have a story to tell you.

About Robert Maxwell and a sheep farmer in North Wales.

A few years ago I had the job of presenting a series of six TV programmes for BBC Wales, all about aristocrats living in Wales, or at least well-established and quite posh families. (It was called *Fine Families,* and was a very strange task for Welsh TV to do, because Wales is such a working-class or rural society that they hardly admit the existence of anything like titles and grandeur on the premises at all. The Scots are big-minded enough to tolerate the sight of a few lords and ladies a-leaping in their kilts, but the Welsh are not.)

One of the families we got involved with, called Price, was not aristocratic so much as grand farming. They had lived in the same nice house in North Wales in the Bala area for three hundred years or more, and owned thousands of acres of sheep farming; the house was full of history, and old family paintings, and relics, and surrounded by landscaped gardens – you can imagine.

One day Mr Price, who knew that I was Fleet Street-based, said to me: 'You might be interested to know that my brother worked for Robert Maxwell. Well, not in the journalistic sense. James is a barrister, and he looked after a lot of Maxwell's cases for him – you know that Maxwell was in the habit of throwing around a lot of libel cases and things?'

I said I did.

'Well, poor old James usually had to pick up the pieces. And one day Maxwell sent for him and said, "James, all these cases I have got on the go, how well are they going to do? How many of them will turn out well for me?" And James had to say in all honesty that he couldn't see any of them turning out well, and that they were all so misjudged that Maxwell was on to losers all along the line. Maxwell said, "Thank you, that is what I wanted to know." And the next day he flew off to his yacht in the Canary Islands, from which he never came back alive.'

'That doesn't prove anything,' I said.

'It's very suggestive,' said Mr Price.

And he was right.

Love,
Miles

Assassination – 4

Dear Gill,

So there we have it.

The murder menu reads as follows.

I would be happy to consider any of the following possibilities:

1. I could murder a real-life person and then write a book about it. (Incidentally, I have just thought of one new late candidate. Wayne Rooney. I have nothing against the lad, but it would be SO tempting to eliminate someone who still has three autobiographies left to write, before he – or is it Hunter Davies? – even begins to write them.)

2. We could revive a real murder and blame it on an old embittered man. (Is there any juicy murder that might in real life have been committed by Robert Maxwell himself?!)

3. I could write a boring old crime novel.

4. I could write a self-help book for senior citizens

who want to commit a murder. I feel that there is very little on the market which is of practical help at all. Perhaps we could license a name well-known in the field, as in 'The Dr Shipman Guide to Family Disposal ...'

Love,
Miles

Assassination – 5

Dear Gill,

Before I entirely leave the subject of Nick Carter, my late father-in-law, who will go down in history as the man who never murdered Colonel Gaddafy, I must tell you about our great day out together.

Nick moved to Africa in the early 1950s and I never met him till we went out to South Africa to stay with him and his wife, Caroline's stepmother, Gillian, some time in the 1980s. He had never been back to Britain in all that time. But we persuaded him to come back for a trip to the old place and duly he came to stay with us in our house in Wiltshire, down in the old English countryside, where he was able to indulge in his passion for all things Arthurian. All things Arthurian are, as far as I can make out, pretty dodgy and fake, but that never worried him on his days out to places like Cadbury Castle and Glastonbury Tor, Avebury, Silbury Hill and Stonehenge. There is nothing Arthurian at all about sites such as Avebury or Stonehenge, of course, but it's still more ancient British than anything in South Africa, except perhaps, he told me, the mid-morning coffee society in Knysna.

(Modern Britain was not of great interest to him. 'Nothing much has changed,' he said, looking round Britain after thirty years absence. I think he was being ironic. I hope he was.)

Before he arrived here from South Africa, I asked him if there was anything he specially wanted to do, or see, or visit, or revisit. Yes, he said, he had a particular list of requirements. There were three of them. He wanted to taste spotted dick again, an old British school pudding he had not eaten in many years. He wanted to go on a genuine steam railway. And he was desperate to meet his favourite writer, Auberon Waugh, whose wide-ranging, caustic wit and sardonic nature were right up his street.

I could not see steam trains being much of a problem. You never seem to be further than fifty miles in England from the nearest tiny working steam railway, although the railway lines themselves are seldom as long as ten miles. Spotted dick would sort itself out. But Auberon Waugh ...

I traded on a passing acquaintanceship to ring him up and put him in the picture. Bron was affability himself. (Did I know him well enough to call him Bron? I am not sure I did. But then, perhaps nobody ever called him anything else.)

'If he is staying with you in Wiltshire,' said Bron, 'the easiest thing for you would be to bring him over for a cup of tea to Combe Florey one Saturday or Sunday afternoon. Just let us know when you're coming and I'll get two extra cups out.'

Combe Florey, the Waugh house, was the other end of Somerset from us, not far from the hilltop town with castle called Dunster. To my amazement, I discovered that the West Somerset Railway, the longest steam railway in Britain, runs right past the Waugh house, from Bishop's Lydeard down to Minehead, so if we did a trip on the railway in the afternoon and then went to see Auberon Waugh for tea … There seemed to be a rather nice old-fashioned hotel in Dunster called the Luttrell Arms, so I rang up and booked a table for lunch there, and we were all set. Especially as I found out, quite by coincidence, that they had spotted dick on the pudding menu that day for lunch.

So by teatime we had achieved two out of three objectives, and I was feeling quite dizzy with smugness. We turned up at Chateau Waugh and knocked on the big front door. The door opened and Bron ushered us into a big room full of dogs rushing round excitedly. They were all Pekinese.

'I hope you don't mind Pekinese,' said Waugh. 'Some people can't stand them. We have a bit of a thing about them in the family.'

167

'On the contrary,' said Nick. 'They are my favourites. When I was working in wildlife conservation in Africa, I trained lots of pekes as hunting dogs. They were wonderful. Saved my life.'

Instead of letting this dribble past him, Bron took in every word and then did something quite marvellous. He turned to everyone else in the room, mostly family getting ready to be dutiful and polite and said: 'Sit down, everyone! There is a man here who has trained pekes as hunting dogs! We will never get the chance to hear how it is done again, so I suggest we listen to what he has to say.'

I did not know this, but Nick's lecture on how to train pekes for survival in the African bush was one of his old star turns, and the Waugh family, and I, and Bron, listened spellbound as he told us why Pekinese dogs are the goods. The reason is partly that they are fearless and partly that things like leopards and cheetahs and lions have never seen a peke before.

'A cheetah isn't really afraid of anything,' said Nick. 'Certainly not anything of its own size. Why would it be? It can outrun anything. But a peke is quite an unknown quantity. It's small and spitting and brave and has no meat on it, and if it advances snarling on a cheetah, a cheetah is going to back off from this little parcel of fury, just to be safe. So when I was out in the bush camping, the last thing I would do before retiring for the night was put a couple of pekes out to roam the bush, and you could guarantee that come morning I had spent a good night's sleep. Anything big out there had kept well clear. Oh, and being so small, a peke could fit into the pocket of a safari jacket, so by day I often carried a peke in each big pocket, a bit like a cowboy carrying a couple of pistols, ready for the draw. Could be quite useful, too. I remember one time …'

It was one of the most successful mini-lectures I have ever heard, and although we eventually got round to tea-time chit-chat and Nick allowed himself to flatter the great Bron, I think that when we drove away from Combe Florey, Nick knew that he had been the main hit.

'I think that went down quite well,' he said.

'You were brilliant,' I said.

'It usually goes well,' he said. 'The only time it failed utterly was when we were having dinner with some Afrikaners and I told them the whole story, and when I was out of the room, I hear the husband say, "I don't believe what Mr Carter is saying. How could he ever get a peke in his pocket? It's far too big!" This baffled me till I realised that the way the Afrikaners say "peke" is identical with the way they pronounce "pig", so he actually thought I had been talking about training pigs for the bush! Stupid man …'

'Actually,' I said, 'I misheard something you said this afternoon. When you were talking about the creatures kept at bay by your Pekinese, I thought that instead of leopards, you said that they drove off "lepers" lurking in the dark.'

I only meant it as a slightly bad taste joke, but Nick for a moment was quite alarmed.

'Lord, I don't want to give that sort of impression,' he said. 'Do you think it is too late to turn round and go back and tell Auberon Waugh I said leopards, not lepers?'

'Yes, I do,' I said, and we drove home.

Love,
Miles

A Children's Book

Dear Gill,

'What's wrong with Daddy, Mummy?'

'Ssshh, dear. Daddy's dying of cancer.'

'What does that mean?'

'Well, sometimes the cells in our body start misbehaving, and instead of reproducing normally, they actually start eating each other …'

Hmm. That's not quite right yet. But it might be on the right lines. The thing is, as we have all been told over the years, children's literature has become more and more capable of tackling grown-up problems, and if you are a teenager who wants to get another view of drugs, or sex, or bereavement, or the meaning of life, you only have to turn to … to …

Anne Fine?

Melvyn Burgess?

Jacqueline Wilson?

Philip Pullman?

Apparently, all these writers have hit the right

wavelength with teenage preoccupations, so if you are a troubled teenager – and what other kind is there? – all you have to do is get the right novel and hear a comforting voice talking about the things that worry *you*, and about the real-life problems that have arrived unbidden on your doorstep.

Not being a troubled teenager, I have never explored this territory, and when I *was* a troubled teenager, there was nothing to help you. You didn't turn to James Bond books to find help with growing up. Conan Doyle, Walter Scott and Alfred Duggan and Co. didn't have a lot to say about teenage angst either. They certainly didn't dole out much advice on how to deal with acne, binge drinking and selling one's memoirs before reaching the tender age of 21. Nor did Richmal Crompton deal with bed-wetting, or take a sympathetic view of childhood obesity.

And yet, Gill, we now know children's literature is an area ripe for exploitation.

And for making a fortune.

It's all there – the baddy aliens (the cancer cells, of course) arrive, unannounced, and go for a takeover. The silent, flesh-eating aliens are undetected. Then some alert radiologist spots the wriggling monsters and Zap! – out comes the chemo-weaponry and war is declared. We know they have their base somewhere in the pancreas and we're sending in our best men to flush it out. On another front, the battle of the liver is raging – our troops are fighting to the death. Oops, now the lungs have been invaded …

It's the sort of thing my son Adam watches on video all the time.

It would make a great picture book. Remember *Fungus the Bogeyman*?

What do you think, Gill, am I on to something?

Love,
Miles

Map

Dear Gill,

It used to be the custom, especially with old-fashioned crime novels, to have a map on the endpapers, usually of the village where the murder had been committed. Little drawings of the manor house. A big X in the woods marked 'Body found here'. There would be a crossroads, a doctor's surgery, the pub, the pond and everything …

I would like a map like that on the endpapers of my book about cancer. The village in the map would not be mentioned at all in the book, it would just be there for decoration and puzzlement. It would have little features like a house marked 'Where the entire book club membership was found dead' and a lych gate labelled 'Only lych gate in Britain licensed for sale of alcohol'.

It would be just a fancy. It would parallel the idea of the index I was going to compose for my autobiography, were I ever to write it, in which all the entries would be vaguely plausible, such as:

'Wogan, Terry, asks Miles Kington to hold his tongue during the climax of the 2001 Eurovision Song Contest, 196.'

Though of course they would all be made up.

I think *Wind in the Willows* and the Christopher Robin books all had endpaper maps like that, which used to captivate me. I could wander in them for hours. The first edition of *War and Peace* also had a huge family tree of all the characters, which was the same kind of thing, but which totally defeated me, and I have still never read it.

Actually, that's all wrong. It would be a map of guts – liver, bile duct, tubing, pancreas, etc. But labelled 'Body found here', 'Vicar's house', 'Major Courtney's house', 'Abandoned car', etc. What do you think?

Love,
Miles

The Will to Live

Dear Gill,

Here's an idea …

One of the cancer specialists at the hospital told me that statistically my chances of getting through another year were not great.

'But statistics are misleading,' he said. 'You could be the exception who goes on and on. I have seen it happen. It all depends on your will to live.'

'How's my will to live?' I said.

'I've no idea,' he said. 'That's up to you.'

I was amazed.

I was so used to having tests done on everything that I assumed there'd be a test for that as well.

If they take blood from you, they can test the blood for almost everything – iron level, genes, bilirubin, whatever the man needs to know.

Why not the will to live?

So, Gill, *Test Your Own Will to Live!* Why not?

Love,
Miles

Yodelling – 1

Dear Gill,

I am afraid that when I first wrote to you some while back suggesting the idea of writing *A Hundred Things to Do Before You Die*, by Miles Kington, a guide to a hundred basic enjoyable techniques to be learnt in your own home, I may have conveyed the false impression that I already knew how to do them.

In this book, for instance, I blithely said I will enable the purchaser to master the art of doing a handstand.

Did you really think I knew how to do a handstand?

Of course not.

But it doesn't take long to work out how to teach it.

If you can show someone how to do a handstand, the fact that you can't do it yourself is not that important.

And something quite miraculous has actually happened since I wrote that letter to you.

I have learnt how to do one of the things that

I thought I could not do.

I have learnt how to yodel.

It came about like this.

In the village where I live, there is a very sociable pub which is a great place to drink at, and also, if you know how to avoid the pitfalls on the menu, a good place for a quick meal. It's old and stone-built, and wood-panelled, and apart from the artificial log fire is pretty olde-worlde. It once became briefly famous when the makers of *The Remains of the Day* used it as a setting for one of the scenes in that film, but as seeing that film is one of the thousands of things I still haven't done, I have no idea how recognisable or even attractive the Hop Pole is in *The Remains*.

It attracts tourists at the weekend. On Fridays there is a gathering of most of the jolly middle-class inhabitants of the village, people like, well, me. During the rest of the week it seems to attract the genuine local inhabitants who would prefer to avoid the jolly middle-class Friday congregation, but also, which is rather odd, it attracts the more adventurous guests from the hotel across the road.

This hotel is a big Victorian pile which might have been a boarding school or a hydro once, but which now survives mostly on coach parties from the Midlands and up North, doing a three-day tour of the West Country, that sort of thing. At the end of the week you see coaches sliding with great difficulty up the village street and into the hotel drive, full of passengers blinking out through the windows and saying: 'Where the hell are we?' (I think this is because quite often the first leg of the journey is described as 'overnighting in Bath', and wherever the coach is arriving it is clearly not in Bath. Not that far from Bath, perhaps. Near Bath, possibly. In a small village five miles from Bath, across the country border in Wiltshire, definitely …)

When the guests get bored with living in a vast Victorian pile, they pop across the road to the pub for a drink, if they have got any initiative, which is how I have found myself striking up conversations with people from as far afield as Ireland, Essex and Japan.

One night I met a pair from Switzerland, who were sitting at the adjacent table in the pub and looked lonely. I love chatting to lonely people. Either I amuse and charm them, or I bore them silly, and then they value their own company when I leave them alone twice as much as they had done ten minutes previously. In this case, they wanted advice on the local beers, so I gave it, and then we had a desultory chat about Swiss politics, and then I told them I had always wanted to know how to yodel. It was the only thing about Switzerland I could think of to say.

'Yodelling is not so difficult,' said the man. 'We all learn it at school in Switzerland. Everyone has to.

It is a tradition, like you having to learn how to sing your national anthem or play chestnuts.'

'Conkers,' said his wife, who turned out to be English.

'Conkers,' he said.

'I cannot see how it is done,' I said. 'Yodelling, I mean. That break in the voice.'

'Like this,' he said.

And, very softly, he sang some Swiss folk song which went from ordinary to falsetto and back so easily …

'What you do is this,' he said, and he showed me the little trick with the throat which I can now put in my book, and which works, every time.

'Can you do it?' I asked his wife, while he was up at the bar buying us all a drink.

'No,' she said. 'Why would I want to yodel? What is the point? I am only married to a Swiss. If yodelling is needed in the family, I can always turn to him. Maybe if there was a Swiss nationality test for immigrants, I might have to learn, but … Come to think of it, why do *you* want to know how to yodel?'

Well, I might have said, because I have suggested an idea to my agent for writing a book on a hundred things to do before you die, like handstands and cart-wheels and things, and yodelling was also on the list, but I thought it would be hard to explain convincingly, and I changed the subject.

I didn't even think about it again for a few days until I was out with the dog, strolling down the field, and suddenly remembered my yodelling lesson. I tried it to see if I could remember. And I could. I could! That little trick with the throat – I remembered it! (I know that proper writers should never use the exclamation mark, but how many proper writers ever got this close to yodelling?)

The next few times I was out with the dog, I tried my yodelling, and I found that I remembered how to do it from time to time. It even started getting better. Of course, it was an ideal place to practise. Nobody could hear me. All I had to compete with was the rest of nature – passing seagulls, magpies, occasional distant trains and cars – and by and large I had this field to myself to make as much noise in as I wanted to. People in Switzerland have whole mountains to practise in, I guess, but I suppose that's why they yodel in the first place, to get heard across vast distances. You'd only invent something like the Alpine horn or the didgeridoo in a wide open space …

The dog looked at me oddly on the first day, but then took it for granted, so by the time I had worked out a little yodelling routine, I just let it belt out. The secret of musical practice is mindless repetition, so I just repeated my exercise mindlessly, until one day I got the shock of my life.

'That's very good,' a voice said.

I hadn't noticed the walker behind me, coming up fast without a dog.

'No, it's not,' I said, confused. 'Sorry about that. I was just practising my … yodelling.'

'I know,' he said. 'that was what was so good about it. You don't often meet people who can yodel.'

Should I have told him that I was only just learning myself?

That I had just met a Swiss bloke in a pub?

Who had taught me one trick?

Of course not.

It would have been inhuman to disdain his praise.

I just preened myself, and said, well, I had the knack, and it was coming on, but it wasn't that difficult, etc., etc., etc.

What I didn't know was that this man lived locally, in a big village not far away, and he was one of the leading spirits on the amateur dramatic society.

At that moment they were planning their Christmas production.

They had decided to do a new version of the William Tell story.

A very jolly version, from the sound of it, halfway between a pantomime, a musical and a James Bond yarn.

The one big snag they had encountered so far

was that nobody in the company knew how to yodel, so they were desperate to find someone who could teach them how to do it.

And it looked as if they had now found one!

I'll let you know how it goes.

Love,
Miles

Yodelling – 2

Dear Gill,

I am in trouble, and I need your help as soon as possible.

The thing is, that I went along to a meeting of the William Tell company, and they seemed satisfied with my yodelling tuition, even though none of them picked it up immediately. What impressed them even more, though, was the fact that I am a professional writer. Some of them had even heard of me, and when you have heard of a writer, you automatically assume they must be good at what they do.

It then transpired that although they have fully committed themselves to doing the William Tell story, they do not as yet have a script.

It has now been put to me that I would be the ideal person to do a script for them.

Less than two months after meeting a Swiss man in a pub, I have been offered a commission to write a full-length evening's entertainment based on William Tell.

The terms, briefly, are, delivery as soon as possible, and no money to change hands at all, because they have no writing budget.

Your task, as my agent?

GET ME OUT OF IT!

I cannot write plays and structured pieces.

I cannot do this.

I am not good at saying no.

You are good at saying no.

Please say yes.

Love,
Miles

A Further Conversation With My Doctor

Dear Gill,

I went to see my oncologist in hospital earlier this week, and we talked about this and that, and the importance of catching cancer early, which I found a bit annoying as they had not caught my cancer early, but it turned out he was just filling in time and wanted to talk to me about something quite different.

'Miles,' he said, which he only calls me when we have moved on to safe topics, 'tell me, are you still writing your book? The book about cancer you mentioned before?'

'Yes,' I said. 'Well, I am still firing some ideas at my agent …'

'Ah!' he said. 'So you have an agent, then?'

'Yes,' I said.

'Good,' he said, and then stopped.

'Is that all?' I said.

'Yes,' he said.

Then he shook his head.

'No,' he said. 'Look, the thing is, I have been writing this book of mine on cancer for several years now, looking at all the new treatments that have come along, because I know a lot about cancer and I think I have got the material for a really good book about it. But I am not good about publishing books, and I don't know how to set about it.'

'Well,' I said, 'it's the same for everyone, really. You get a good idea. You do some writing. You get an agent interested, and the agent then gets some publisher interested ...'

'Hold on there!' said the oncologist. 'You've missed out a vital bit of information there!'

'Have I?'

'Yes. You haven't mentioned the name of the agent.'

'Oh. Sorry. What is the name of the agent?'

'I don't know,' said the oncologist. 'I only know about cancer. You're the one that knows about books and agents.'

Slowly, a kind of greeny, dim light began to dawn.

What was happening was that my oncologist was appealing to me for help with his book.

He seemed to think that I might be able to help him get his book published.

A diabolical sort of bargain was in the offing

whereby he would advise me about cancer while in return I would …

'Look, Dr Benton … ,' I said.

'Call me David,' he said.

'Is David your name?' I said, surprised.

He didn't seem like a David to me.

He seemed a little doubtful himself.

'I'll just check,' he said.

He turned to his desk and tapped away at his computer. This is one thing I have discovered this year about the NHS and indeed all hospital-based medicine nowadays, that the doctor feels he has to check everything with his computer and his database before he quite dares say or do anything. That little screen in the corner is the key to all he needs to know. As long as he can remember how to access it.

'Oh, dear,' he said. 'I think I've forgotten my password again. I had to change it before I went on holiday last time, and I keep forgetting what the new one is.'

'David,' I said.

'Yes?' he said.

'No,' I said. 'I am wondering if your new password might not be David.'

'Oh, of course. Yes, it is,' he said. 'How on earth did you know that?'

'People quite often choose their own name for their password,' I said. 'It's very unsafe, but they do.'

Having established that his name was David, Dr Benton now turned his attention back to the missing agent, and to try to establish a name for them as well, which he thought I had the key to.

'You see,' he said, 'if only I had the right agent, I think this book on cancer would be a winner.'

There then followed five minutes of close fencing, in the course of which he as good as suggested that I put him in touch with you, and I as good as suggested that my doing so would endanger our relationship for all time.

'Have you not heard of the Euroclitic Oath?' I said, improvising desperately.

'Euroclitic? What's that?'

'It's the sacred oath which all writers have to sign with their agents.'

'Like the Hippocratic Oath?'

'Oh, much more serious than that,' I said. 'It involves …'

I was about to tell him that it involved cutting your wrist slightly and then mingling your life bloods, until I realised that he would not find this at all impressive as doctors did that kind of thing all day long, often merely by accident.

'It involves swapping bank account numbers and exchanging vital financial fluids, and things like that,' I said.

He looked revolted.

'Well,' he said,' do you think that if you consulted your agent, he might put me on to the right person?'

'She.'

'What?'

'Not a he. A she.'

'Your agent is a woman?'

I had an overwhelming temptation to say, 'I'll check,' turn to a computer in the corner and access a database to make sure you were a woman, but unfortunately I hadn't got a computer with me.

'Yes,' I said.

'I see,' he said.

I don't know what he meant by that.

That is how things stand at the moment.

If you don't mind, I would rather not put him in touch with you.

I am happy for you to get a bestseller on cancer published, but I would much rather it were by me than by my oncologist.

Tell me you agree.

And remember the old Euroclitic Oath which binds us so closely.

Love,
Miles

Afterword
by Caroline Kington

Miles Kington was born in Northern Ireland in 1941, grew up in North Wales, and was sent away to school in Scotland, but he saw himself very much as an Englishman (although to complicate matters further, he was actually half American, his mother being a U.S. citizen).

'From an early age, perhaps confused by my shifting geography,' he once wrote, 'I knew I wanted to be a humorous writer and a jazz musician, and even at school I had already started my own jazz band and set up a humorous magazine in opposition to the official school magazine. When I went to Oxford University (1960–63, studying French and German), I spent most of the time playing the double bass in jazz groups and writing undergraduate humour. Thus when I left university I was almost entirely unfitted for life, and consequently went to London to try my luck as a free-lance humorous writer, where I nearly starved to death.'

Miles set his sights on joining *Punch*, a humorous magazine famed for its cartoons and the quality of its writing, a magazine no doctor's or dentist's waiting room was without. He bombarded them with articles, till they finally gave in and allowed him to join the staff.

Whilst at *Punch* he created the 'Let's Parler Franglais' columns, which led to four volumes with Penguin, which he described as 'probably the most popular bilingual lavatory books of the 1980s.' *Franglais* remains a firm favourite with the British today, poking fun, as it does, at the Brits' determined inability to speak any other language.

Miles had a deep passion for jazz and was the jazz reviewer of *The Times* newspaper (London) for fifteen years. He played the piano and the double bass, and joined the cabaret group Instant Sunshine as their bass player. By the 1980s he was making regular appearances on British television and radio, but he eschewed a potentially glittering career on television because, he said, it got in the way of his writing, something he was single-minded about.

Writers whom he particularly admired and who influenced him greatly, certainly in the earlier days, were H. L. Mencken, S. J. Perelman, and a nineteenth-century French humorist named Alphonse Allais, whose work he translated and had published under the title *A Wolf in Sheep's Clothing*, the first of many books. In addition to the four *Franglais* books, Miles wrote *Nature Made Ridiculously Simple*, *Steaming Through Britain*, *Moreover*, *Moreover Too*, *Miles and Miles*, *Welcome to Kington*, *The Jazz Anthology*, *The Franglais Lieutenant's Woman*, and *Motorway Madness*, as well as editing books on Harry Graham and Ruthless Rhymes, the cartoonist Sempé, and several collections from *Punch*.

In 1980 Miles left *Punch* and joined the staff of *The Times* newspaper under the editorship of Harry Evans, where he wrote a daily humorous column, 'Moreover,' until 1987, when he switched to *The Independent*, where he wrote daily until he died, in 2008. Quite apart from all the other articles he wrote and all the books, he had written over 4,500 humorous articles.

One hesitates to use that tired old word *unique*, but the fact that he wrote a humorous column every day marked him out as a colossus in British journalism (described as such by Simon Kelner, editor of *The Independent*). His fellow hacks regarded his output with awe and, to date, no-one has taken his place.

He lived to write, and it was entirely apt his last column appeared on the day he died.

Miles wrote because he found words endlessly fascinating. He was a humorist because he loved playing with them, making language stand on its head to look at life's experiences in a different, tangential, and oblique way. His writing provided a different perspective, one that made readers smile, laugh, and see things afresh. But although he was well known in Britain for *Franglais* and his columns, he wanted to leave something more substantial behind for posterity.

For years Gill Coleridge, his agent, and I tried to persuade him to write his autobiography. He'd met so many interesting people, through *Punch*, through broadcasting, and as part of the jazz scene; and, as a permanently curious person, he had so much information tucked away in that enormous brain of his. He never entirely dismissed the idea, but thought that it might be something he would do when he retired. As if!

About five years before he died, Miles succumbed to pressure and sat down ostensibly to write his autobiography. The book, published as *Someone Like Me*, was a masterpiece of humorous fiction from beginning to end.

He had just started writing the sequel, *Here We Go Again*, when he was diagnosed with pancreatic cancer. Time was running out. He abandoned the book and started writing a series of fictitious letters, ostensibly to Gill, proposing ways in which he could turn his battle with cancer into a best-seller. As he had intended, these letters *were* the book, and *How Shall I Tell the Dog?* became his last project.

Writing the book as a series of letters suited his style of writing. He was not a long-haul writer, and the idea of undertaking a conventional novel appalled him. No, he was a brilliant short-story writer, because that's what his columns, by and large, are. 'The Gods,' 'The Pub Conversations,' 'Nature Rambles with Uncle Geoffrey,' 'One Minute Detective,' to name but a few of his regular favorites, are all stories, characters, conveyed within seconds with wonderfully easy dialogue. And we all—family, friends, neighbours, even our beloved spaniel, Berry—became characters in those stories.

Everything Miles wrote, even thank-you letters, notes to the milkman or the window cleaner, or late-night instructions for our teenage son, Adam—don't forget to lock up, turn the lights out, etc.—reflected his sense of fun.

Here's an example:

Adam—tonight a letter with a difference, i.e.
written by your father and still legible. Nice fresh
bread tonight, and a mouth-watering choice of
sandwich fillings.
BEEF, GARLIC SAUSAGE, CHEESE 'N' HAM
And also please indicate your preferred mode of
travel to work tomorrow
TRAIN___
CAR___
If you wish to have dreams tonight, please indicate
your preferred choice of subject matter
SPY DRAMA___
EROTIC TALES___
ANCIENT MYTHS___
EXTREMELY TENSE ATTEMPT TO DRIVE ROUND
    SMALL BACK STREET IN OXFORD___
Note: Not all dream themes may be available

It follows, therefore, that when Miles was diagnosed with cancer, there was no way he would not write about it, and that, devastating though it was, it would be given the same treatment as anything else he'd ever written about.

Writing about it helped him, not to come to terms with it, exactly, but in the same way people are encouraged to talk and not brood, Miles wrote. One could say he found writing cathartic, and so cancer became a scenario, a situation he could view almost dispassionately, winkle out the quirky elements, find the humour, turn tragedy into comedy, neutralise the fear.

Ironically, setting out to be a series of fictitious letters, *How Shall I Tell The Dog?* is actually the most autobiographical of his writings, embracing as it does not only the cancer but other real happenings in Miles's life, too.

He was very disciplined—even on days when he felt pretty dreadful. He wrote his column first, and then any energy left over was given to the Letters to Gill. In the early stages, he would write directly into the computer. As he grew weaker, sitting at his desk became more and more uncomfortable, so he resorted to lying on a daybed in front of the fire, the dog his constant companion, and writing longhand, transferring what he'd written to the keyboard when he felt strong enough.

The book is divided into three sections: Facing the Mountain, Crossing the Plateau, and The Descent. The surgeon who first confirmed the diagnosis described the progress of the disease in these terms. Miles liked that, although it did provide us with some confusion. 'Am I facing the mountain or is this the descent?' he would ask, on days he didn't feel that well.

In the event, the plateau wasn't quite as wide as we had hoped and the descent was quicker and he is no longer here. But the book is. And above all else, he would want people to read it and not mourn his departure but laugh at the telling of it.

—March 2009

Index

10/09